grilled cheese, please!

grilled cheese, please!

50 Scrumptiously Cheesy Recipes

LAURA WERLIN

PHOTOGRAPHS BY MAREN CARUSO

**Andrews McMeel
Publishing, LLC**

Kansas City • Sydney • London

Andrews McMeel Publishing, LLC
an Andrews McMeel Universal company
1130 Walnut Street, Kansas City, Missouri 64106

www.andrewsmcmeel.com

13 14 15 16 17 WKT 10 9 8 7 6 5 4 3 2 1

ISBN: 978-1-4494-4735-9

Library of Congress Control Number: 2010930550

This 2013 edition printed exclusively for Barnes & Noble, Inc.

Design: Ren-Whei Harn and Holly Ogden
Photography: Maren Caruso
Digital/Photo Assistant: Christina Richards
Food Stylist: Kim Kissling
Food Stylist Assistant: Abby Stolfo

www.laurawerlin.com

Attention: Schools and Businesses
Andrews McMeel books are available at quantity discounts with bulk purchase for educational, business, or sales promotional use. For information, please e-mail the Andrews McMeel Publishing Special Sales Department: specialsales@amuniversal.com

Contents

Acknowledgments

Were it not for the following people, this book would not be. It's that simple, and I'm that lucky.

As always, my heartfelt thanks goes to my magnificent agent and friend, Carole Bidnick, without whose persistence this book would have remained just an idea. The Andrews McMeel dream team consisting of my ace editor, Jean Lucas, and incredible publisher, Kirsty Melville, helped take my vision light years beyond my own imagination, and I am over the moon with the results. I thank you both.

Also among dream teams, photographer Maren Caruso, food stylist Kim Kissling, and their assistants Abby Stolfo and Christina Richards once again created the best food photos of anyone in the business. My deepest gratitude also to Heather Porter-Engwall and the Wisconsin Milk Marketing Board for supplying the great Wisconsin cheeses for those photos as well.

I shudder to think where I would have been without my amazing recipe tester, Sheri Castle, who brought these recipes from good to great thanks to her dedication and extreme competence. Likewise, my unofficial recipe tester and extraordinary friend, Lynne Devereux, added extra insurance by applying her formidable cooking skills along with her knowledge and passion for cheese to whip a few recipes into shape.

My heartfelt appreciation goes to the following people for reasons too many to count. To Karen Martin, who knows no bounds to friendship and offered research help when her own book needed tending; to Linda and Kelly Hayes, who ate countless grilled cheese sandwiches in the name of experimentation and somehow still managed to smile; to chef Ryan Hardy, who eked out recipes when he had absolutely no time to do so; to Sam Beall and the folks at Blackberry Farm who not only supplied the wonderful recipe for pimento cheese (page 119), but more importantly gave me a safe haven at their incredible property to begin this book; to Kathleen Weber, owner of the unparalleled bakery Della Fattoria in Sonoma County, who handed me loaf after loaf of her amazing bread to play with for my grilled cheese sandwich recipe development; to Tami Parr and Flavio de Castilhos for indulging my need to try the Cheesus Burger at The Grilled Cheese Grill in Portland; and to my cousins Kim and Miles Keilin for happily eating my iteration of same. Thanks also to Valerie Henderson, Anita Ettinger, Joyce Goldstein, Beth Roemer, Faye Keogh, Kevin Donahue, Aggie Skirball, and Dipti Anderson for their great palates and friendships. To Mom and Dad, "thank you" will never be a sufficient phrase.

Finally, I must thank the following two people who have shaped me professionally and personally forever. The first is my former editor Julie Stillman. Although no longer editing, she is someone who made each author she worked with a little better, and I, for one, will always be grateful for her skill and wisdom. The other is my loyal and incomparably kind sister, Andi, who not only embraces all my projects with enthusiasm but who also contributes to them in ways even she does not know. And so I tell her now.

Introduction

Even Pavlov didn't know the power of grilled cheese. If he had, he would have gone straight for the sandwich instead of the bell to evoke the cascade of visceral responses, like hunger pangs, salivary glands gone wild, and an irrepressible smile that follow its mere mention.

Say *grilled cheese* and the memories of a childhood indulgence, the first cooking lesson from Mom or Dad, a bowl of tomato soup, or the aroma of melting cheese comes wafting into consciousness. And it doesn't stop there. The two words strung together also bring to mind seductive images of the sound of bread sizzling and crackling as it makes its transformation from soft and pillowy to butter-crisped and crunchy. These imagined sights and sounds tease with anticipation, because just knowing that as the bread turns golden brown the strands of cheese nestled within are languorously but ever so surely giving way to their melted glory.

Whoever thought that the most basic of sandwiches, the one we all grew up with, the one that was the easy solution for Mom instead of a full meal, the one we all loved but didn't really pay much attention to, the sandwich that combined nondescript bread and even less notable cheese, would today become the subject of recipe contests and blogs, the focal point of entire restaurants, the inspirational fuel that fires up mobile food trucks, and the basic foundation on which Americans build their ideal of the *best* grilled cheese sandwich? Grilled cheese, the movement, has arrived.

Indeed, it appears that the grilled cheese phenomenon is dovetailing with the entire food movement in America. With *natural*, *local*, and *artisan* now rolling off the tongue the way *TV dinners* did in the 1960s, the not-so-humble grilled cheese sandwich falls in lockstep with today's way of eating. Sources of farmhouse cheese and artisan bread are more plentiful than ever. Grilled cheese add-ins like bacon, tomatoes, vegetables, ham, and fruit, and a seemingly infinite number of other filling choices, now include details on their labels explaining their provenance, the degree to which the product is "natural" or possibly even organic, and so on. Because of this, making grilled cheese sandwiches today allows us the guilty pleasure of satisfying our hunger needs while simultaneously appeasing our inner locavore.

Why This Book?

Although I already memorialized 50 grilled cheese recipes in another book, grilled cheese has grown up since that book was published. Or at least it has in my house. But that's not the only place: Judging by the fact that national television morning shows devote segments to it during National Grilled Cheese month (April), the blogosphere sports sites dedicated exclusively to it (along with no small amount of reverence for it), and even fast-food restaurants are now in on the act, I'd say the *new* grilled cheese sandwich has arrived. And it's decidedly not our mother's version.

When I judged the 1st 8th Annual Grilled Cheese Invitational in Los Angeles in April 2010 (don't ask why it's called the "1st 8th"), it pretty much rocked my world. Not only was I exposed to more combinations involving cheese between two slices of grilled bread than I'd ever imagined (including a few I hope never to see again, alas), I was also blown away by the fervor of the 250 competitors and the 8,000 attendees. All this for grilled cheese? That sealed the deal. I had to craft my own versions of this new/old sandwich as well as incorporate those from some grilled cheese–crazy friends, chefs, and a few from those responsible for fueling the trend by way of their stand-alone restaurants and mobile food trucks. What greater respect for this exalted sandwich than to open a business based on it? And so, this book.

One of the things I learned along my grilled cheese journey is that some of the grilled cheese professionals believe in creating sandwiches that tilt much closer to haute rather than humble cuisine. That's why they have throngs of patrons willing to stand in line and pay money for their sandwiches. You'll find some of their recipes in this book, and believe me, they're great. Just be forewarned that they take a little forethought.

What you'll also find in this book is everything from basic grilled cheese to exotic, from nostalgic to modern, from ethnic to all-American, from savory to sweet. I'll also share with you the very best method for making grilled cheese sandwiches. Sure, you can do it any way you want, but why not strive for foolproof if you can? If you use my method, I promise you'll get crisp bread and perfectly melted cheese every time.

You also might want to know the best breads for grilled cheese and, of course, the best cheeses. You'll find that here. You'll also find out whether it's best to spread butter, use mayo, or brush oil on the bread; what kind of pan to cook it in; and how to make it on the stovetop or in a sandwich maker. Almost everybody salivates at the thought of tomato soup with grilled cheese, and while you'll find a recipe for grilled tomato soup here, you might want to expand your grilled cheese go-with horizons. Deep-fried pickles, anyone?

In some ways, grilled cheese needs no explanation, no elaboration, no exacting standards. Fundamentally, grilled cheese is about emotional nurturing; it's not a fussy intellectual pursuit. But that doesn't mean you can't take Mom's and do one better. Or for that matter, rather than disparage Mom's cooking, think about improving your own version by way of the pages that follow. I can't make any promises, but I feel pretty certain that you'll be happy with the results.

Now You're Cookin'

The question of how to make the "best" grilled cheese is the subject of some debate among aficionados. But after having made hundreds of them, I'm confident that my method is pretty much foolproof. Here it is in a nutshell:

- Grate the cheese
- Thick (cheese) and thin (bread)
- Spread the bread, not the pan
- Stick with nonstick (mostly)
- Bring out the sandwich maker
- Fire up the (gas) grill
- Cover it
- Flatten slightly
- Go low and slow
- Cool it, then eat it

Why You Should be Grate-ful

Some people quibble with the relative hassle of grating cheese rather than slicing it. I can understand that, but all I can tell you is that if you're going to the trouble of dirtying a pan to make grilled cheese, you'll be handsomely rewarded by taking the few extra seconds to grate the cheese.

When you slice the cheese, you're cutting a solid piece of cheese that will naturally resist melting unless it's so thin it's translucent. Sure, a slice of cheese will eventually melt if it's heated long enough, but in the meantime you're having to watch over the bread like a mother hen to make sure it doesn't burn. Why go through that aggravation when you can avoid it simply by turning your cheese slices into shreds that are practically pre-melted by virtue of their wispiness? Trust me on this.

Ratio Rationale

If a grilled cheese sandwich is made with super-thick slices of bread, it's nearly always doomed. That's because too-thick bread will never achieve the crackly, crisp texture that defines a grilled cheese sandwich. Equally important, if the cheese is encased in thick bread, it has almost no chance of melting thoroughly. This brings about another tenet of successful grilled cheese making: The proper ratio of bread to cheese is crucial for the perfect sandwich.

Flavor the Bread, Not the Pan

A lot of people insist on adding butter or oil to the pan and then placing the sandwich in the pan once it's been heated. The problem with that method is that the minute you put the sandwich in the sizzling pan, the fat you've used to coat the pan will immediately be soaked up by the bread in a random, blotchy manner rather than as an even coat. Not only does this tamp down the overall flavor of the finished sandwich, but it also makes for dry patches of bread. Sure, you can avoid this by adding lots and lots of butter or oil to the pan, but at that point you're making a deep-fried sandwich rather than a grilled one. So spread the bread with your butter or oil instead.

Nonstick versus Cast Iron

This is actually not an either/or situation. The fact is, if you like using a cast-iron pan for your grilled cheese sandwiches, then continue to do so. The reason I stick with nonstick is because it cooks evenly and, of course, it's a breeze to clean. Plus, if you care about such things as using less butter, a nonstick will allow you that freedom. One caveat about nonstick: Use the best-quality pan you can. It will be heavier and will help ensure that your sandwich cooks evenly.

Sandwich Maker Sense

When cooked on a sandwich maker, a grilled cheese sandwich strays from traditional but not from the key flavor and textural components that make this quintessential sandwich great. That's because sandwich makers ensure crisp bread, a perfect bread-to-cheese ratio, and oozy cheese. Another sandwich maker advantage is that although using butter, olive oil, or mayonnaise on the outside of the bread tastes great, you probably don't need to use quite as much when you use a sandwich maker. That's because the weight of the lid of the sandwich maker presses and distributes even the smallest amount of buttered goodness right into the bread. Not a drop is wasted as it might be in a conventional pan. When it comes to that lid, keep in mind that while its weight is helpful to ensure crisp bread, it can also be *too* heavy if the sandwich filling is particularly soft, oozy, or loose to begin with. In that case, consider using the stovetop method instead.

Outdoor Cooking

Grilled cheese sandwiches are nothing if not versatile, including how you cook them. In addition to stovetops and sandwich makers, the outdoor gas grill is perfect for the literal "grilled" cheese sandwich. Just brush the grill rack with a little oil and follow the directions for the stovetop method.

Cover and Cook

You're probably thinking that it makes no sense to cover a grilled cheese sandwich when the goal is to have a crisp outcome. That's a logical supposition, but it turns out it doesn't fly. The reality is that by covering the sandwich during most of the cooking process you're ensuring that every strand of cheese will melt long before the bread has a chance to burn. I promise that the contact between the sandwich and the pan will bring the process to a crisp conclusion—and the payoff is that the gooey factor will be assured.

Flat and Fabulous

One way to achieve the Goldilocks "just right" seal of approval is to be sure to press down on the sandwich during the cooking process. That's the concept behind a sandwich maker, but you don't need to plug anything in to attain the same effect. Instead, all you have to do is use your handy-dandy spatula to press down on the sandwich after you've flipped it.

Another option is to use an aluminum foil–wrapped can of, say, tomatoes or anything else that's heavy. You can try using a foil-wrapped brick, too, but sometimes that's *too* heavy and your filling might squirt out. I might add, though, that if you're using a nonstick pan, all may not be lost in that case. The filling can be retrieved and tucked back in between the slices of bread much more easily than if you're using a cast-iron pan, in which the filling will likely be subjected to an immediate death grip.

As you'll see in the recipes that follow, I instruct you to flip the sandwich not once, but twice. That too is in the service of making sure the bread is crisp and the cheese inside is thoroughly melted. Just consider that little extra flick of the wrist a calorie burner.

Fire 'Em Up (but Not Too High)

One thing is certain: Everybody's BTUs differ. That means that my stove's medium heat is different from yours. In turn, that means that my instructions have to be adapted to your stove. I've learned, though, that medium heat is certainly the safest even if it means waiting a minute or two longer for your mouthwatering creations to cook. If the heat is too high, your bread will burn before your cheese has a chance to melt.

Better to be patient and let the cheese succumb to the heat rather than force it to melt prematurely. By taking a little extra time (I'm talking 2 or 3 minutes, not 20 or 30), you'll achieve the perfect balance of a steamy, melting interior encased in crackly, crisp bread. The same is true when using a sandwich maker. If your sandwich maker has temperature control, you'll probably find that medium to medium-high is the right temperature to ensure crisp bread while melting the cheese inside. If there's no temperature control, don't worry. Just watch carefully. In sum, your watch phrase for the perfect grilled cheese sandwich should be *lower and slower*.

Cool It

Although the following advice may test every fiber of patience in your entire being, I urge you to exercise restraint before eating your sandwich. That is, let it cool for at least 5 minutes before eating it. Why? As a grilled cheese sandwich cools, the flavors brighten—a lot. If the sandwich is too hot, it will be mouth-searing and have little taste.

A Method to the (Grilled Cheese) Madness

Now it's time for the nuts and bolts on bread, cheese, and a few other crucial grilled cheese components.

First, note that **each recipe makes 4 sandwiches**. Feel free to halve the recipes or to double them. Unlike in baking, there's no science involved in altering the quantity in these recipes; there's only math.

Bread: It Matters How You Slice It

One of the things I realized as I prepared these sandwiches is that there's no standard-size piece of bread. That is, your piece of sourdough bread might be different than mine. In turn, that means that the quantity of filling for my bread may be too sparse for yours. Or conversely, it might be too voluminous. For that reason, I created these recipes to fit the typical presliced sandwich bread, or bread that measures 4 to 5 inches wide, 3 to 3½ inches tall, and about ½ inch thick. If your bread is different, you'll have to adjust the filling amount. In almost every case, the adjustment will be minor, and it will usually mean you'll have to scale down.

The one exception to this is if your loaf is round. That's because the center slices will be quite long. In this case, you'll have to cut those long slices in half crosswise. This will create pieces that are fairly close to the typical sandwich-size slice, or slightly smaller.

A sandwich-size slice of bread =
4 to 5 inches wide, 3 to 3½ inches tall, and ½ inch thick

Cheese by the Ounce

As you'll see in the recipes that follow, I specify the number of ounces of cheese you'll need for each recipe. I do this because I figure that when you're at the store you're buying cheese by the ounce, not by the cup. That said, I think it might be helpful for you to know that 4 ounces of coarsely grated cheese is the equivalent of 1½ cups.

4 ounces of coarsely grated cheese
is the equivalent of 1½ cups

Also, when you see the phrase *coarsely grated*, that means that the cheese pieces should be about ¼ inch in diameter, roughly the size of the large holes of a box grater. The term *finely grated* means the cheese should be about the same diameter as a piece of string.

Butter Up!

I've already explained why it's better to butter the bread rather than the pan, but the question now is whether it's better to use butter, mayonnaise, or oil. When I make a grilled cheese sandwich, I almost always have butter nearby. Simply put, butter is best. And not just any butter, but *salted* butter (more on that below). That said, you should let your own preference dictate your choice. If you don't like butter, then by all means, use something else. If you're an equal-opportunity fat lover like I am, then the sandwich ingredients will give you the best clue about which fat to use.

For example, there are a couple of sandwiches in this book that call for olive bread or that use olives in the filling. To me, that's pretty much saying, "Use olive oil rather than butter." It would taste good either way, but it seems more logical to use the oil.

Another word about oil: There is no reason I can think of to use any type other than olive oil for your grilled cheese sandwiches. You don't need to use the extra-virgin stuff, but vegetable oil will almost always be a neutral proposition. That is, it will crisp the bread, but it will lend absolutely no distinction to your sandwich.

As for mayonnaise, very few recipes here call for the creamy egg and oil concoction, but it really is a very good bread-crisper-upper and golden-browner. If you love mayo, then by all means, use it!

When all is said and done, you will find that the majority of recipes in this book call for *salted* butter. Why, you might ask, would I use salted butter when there's already salt in the cheese and perhaps in some of the other sandwich fillings as well? The answer is simple: For the best overall sandwich flavor, the bread needs a little salt too. Salted butter ensures that it gets it.

Worth Its Salt

I use kosher salt as my go-to salt for all my cooking, and the same is true for the recipes in this book. That is, any time you see salt in the ingredient list, know that it means kosher salt. You can use coarse sea salt if you prefer, but bear in mind that it doesn't dissolve as readily and has a tad more minerally flavor than kosher salt.

Cheese, Please

Needless to say, the better the cheese melts, the more your sandwich will ooze with melting goodness. Sounds easy unless you're not sure which cheeses will melt. I'll make it easy for you. Choose any of the ones in the first three categories below and you'll be in good shape. The cheeses in the fourth category make great grilled cheese sandwiches too; they just don't melt. What they do, though, is add loads of flavor. As you'll discover, I call for these cheeses to be used sometimes as flavor enhancers on the *outside* of the bread. Mixed with butter, they create an unbeatable nutty flavor and toasty crust. The final category that follows is just a handful of some of the outstanding artisan cheeses being made in America that also make great melters. A sandwich made with one of these cheeses will transform an ordinary grilled cheese sandwich into a memorable one.

1) Easy-to-find melters

American cheese slices, white or orange
Asiago (fresh, not aged; often referred to as *fresco*)
Cheddar
Colby
Colby-Jack
Fontina
Gouda

Gruyère
Havarti
Monterey Jack
Mozzarella
Provolone (mild or medium, not sharp or extra-sharp)
Swiss (including Jarslberg)
Velveeta (you won't find any recipes calling for Velveeta in this book, but it does belong in the category of serious melters even if it isn't technically cheese)

2) Slightly more exotic melting cheeses

These are cheeses that you're more likely to find in a store with a more extensive cheese selection than just the basics. Some of these have more complex and/or pronounced flavors, which I've indicated with an asterisk.

Appenzeller
Comté*
Emmentaler
Mahón
Manchego (sheep's milk cheese)
Midnight Moon (goat Gouda)
Ossau-Iraty (sheep's milk cheese)
Pecorino (fresh, not aged; often referred to as *fresco*)
Petit Basque (sheep's milk cheese)
Raclette*

3) Cheeses that melt but don't become stretchy

The unstretchable cheeses are those that become creamy (sublime, really), but they'll never create stretchy strands of melting goodness the way, say, mozzarella does. They serve an important purpose in a grilled cheese sandwich, though: adding flavor. It's hard to beat a cheese like melted Brie in just about any context.

Blue cheese (all)

Brie

Camembert

Fromage blanc (a cow's milk cheese similar in texture to fresh goat cheese or ricotta)

Fresh goat cheese

Reblochon (French cheese that can be found in most stores with good cheese selections)

Taleggio (Italian cheese that can be found in most stores with good cheese selections)

4) Nonmelting but nutty cheeses

Asiago (aged)

Dry Monterey Jack

Grana Padano

Mimolette (*vieille*, or aged)

Parmigiano-Reggiano

Pecorino (aged)

Piave Vecchio

SarVecchio

Unique American Artisan (Melting) Cheeses

Beecher's Handmade Cheese "Flagship" (Seattle, Washington)

Beehive Cheese Company "Promontory Cheddar" (Uintah, Utah)

BelGioioso Mild Provolone (Denmark, Wisconsin)

Bellwether Farms "Carmody" (Petaluma, California)

Carr Valley Cheese Company "Marisa" (LaValle, Wisconsin)

Cowgirl Creamery "Wagon Wheel" (Petaluma, California)

Edelweiss Creamery "Emmentaler" (Monticello, Wisconsin)
Emmi-Roth Käse "Grand Cru" Gruyère (Monroe, Wisconsin)
Meadow Creek Dairy "Appalachian" (Galax, Virginia)
Mozzarella Company Mozzarella (Dallas, Texas)
Point Reyes Farmstead Cheese Company Toma (Point Reyes, California)
Rogue Creamery "Touvelle" (Central Point, Oregon)
Saxon Creamery "Big Eds" (Cleveland, Wisconsin)
Sweet Grass Dairy "Thomasville Tomme" (Thomasville, Georgia)
Thistle Hill Farm and Spring Brook Farm "Tarentaise" (North Pomfret and Reading, Vermont)
Tillamook Vintage White Medium Cheddar (Tillamook, Oregon)
Uplands Cheese Company "Pleasant Ridge Reserve" (Dodgeville, Wisconsin)
Vella Cheese Company "Italian Style Table Cheese" (Sonoma, California)
Widmer Cheese Cellars Colby (Theresa, Wisconsin)

Bread: The Best Thing Since Sliced

Although you can use just about any bread you like or have on hand to make a satisfying grilled cheese sandwich, if you expand your bread imagination, you can end up with an extraordinary sandwich, not just a ho-hum one.

Think about it. Isn't the notion of a bread made with lots of butter (as in croissants and brioche); or with goodies in it like olives or walnuts; or hearty like Italian, sourdough, or *pain au levain*; or crusty like ciabatta more enticing than white, wheat, or rye? Don't get me wrong. I love these simple breads for grilled cheese sandwiches too. In fact, you'll find plenty of recipes in this book that call for those mainstay breads. But when it's so easy to gussy up your sandwich just by switching to a more exotic bread, why not do it?

What follows is a list of some of the more unusual breads called for in some of the recipes in this book, along with their easy-to-find substitutions.

CIABATTA: From the Italian word for "slipper," *ciabatta* is, well, shaped like a slipper. Pronounced chuh-BOTT-uh, it is a light yet crusty bread that's pretty much perfect for a grilled cheese sandwich. It's the crust that seals the deal. Unlike heartier breads, ciabatta crust is relatively thin and brittle and encases a soft, airy center. Because of the bread's airy texture, it's easy to pinch out some of the soft center to create a well in the bread, which is important for ensuring the best bread-to-cheese ratio or, in other words, a sandwich that isn't doughy. You'll find ciabatta in its signature flattened loaf shape as well as in individual rolls. The rolls are often in the freezer section. You can use either for the sandwiches in this book.

- If you can't find ciabatta, use Italian bread, sourdough, or baguette.

CROISSANT: Crescent shaped, this light-as-a-feather roll is distinguished by its layers and layers of butter. This is why croissants taste so good. It's also why they make amazing grilled cheese sandwiches. The "built-in" butter means that you'll get plenty of flavor, and equally important, a crisp texture. The bonus is that because of all that butter, croissants succumb to heat easily, which means that when you put a little pressure on them with your spatula, they'll readily compress. The result is a super-crisp exterior and dreamy, creamy melted cheese inside.

- If you can't find croissants, use brioche, egg bread, or challah.

CUBAN ROLL: To be honest, most of us won't have access to a genuine Cuban roll. As far as I know, we have to go to Florida or Cuba or a Cuban bakery to get the real deal. They're not usually shipped because they're best when fresh. Used to make a Cubano (page 87), a Cuban roll looks similar to a baguette in length, but its crust is flakier and the inside is softer. Also, unlike a baguette, Cuban rolls are usually made with lard or some other type of fat. They also have a signature seam down the middle.

- If you can't find Cuban rolls, use crusty sandwich rolls or baguette.

FOCACCIA: Usually rectangular in shape, this Italian bread is soft, almost spongy, in texture and made with lots of olive oil. It will often have herbs such as rosemary added to it, and sometimes garlic as well. For the purposes of the focaccia sandwiches in this book, try to find ones without added herbs or flavorings if you can.

- If you can't find focaccia, use brioche or French bread in loaf size.

ITALIAN BREAD: Although it sounds rather generic, Italian bread, along with sourdough, is my go-to bread for most grilled cheese sandwiches. It has a fairly dense texture (this means not too many holes from which the filling could seep out), a sturdy but not tooth-breaking crust, and a fairly neutral, though by no means boring, flavor. Instead, it has hints of sourness like sourdough, and an overall hearty, almost savory, flavor.

- If you can't find Italian bread, use French bread, *pain de mie*, or country white.

OLIVE BREAD: Just as the words indicate, this type of bread is studded with black olives. Occasionally you'll find olive bread made with green olives or a mixture of both as well. The main thing to keep in mind is that olive breads tend to be denser than many other breads. This means that the cheese between the two slices will take longer to melt. All you have to do is remember low (heat) and slow (cooking), and your sandwich will be perfect.

- If you can't find olive bread, use Italian or sourdough and add a handful of pitted and coarsely chopped black olives, such as kalamata, to the filling.

PAIN DE MIE: Pretty much identical to a Pullman loaf, *pain de mie* is good old-fashioned white bread with a light but closed-texture interior (read: no large holes) and a thin crust. It's made in a loaf shape with squared-off rather than rounded corners, and for that reason it is perfect for sandwiches.

- If you can't find *pain de mie* or Pullman, use country white bread or white bread.

PAIN AU LEVAIN: Don't be intimidated by the French phrase. Just know that it translates to utter goodness. Not literally, but *pain au levain* is made with a bacterial starter that, when combined with yeast, creates a slow-rising, sour (as in sourdough), hearty bread. It is usually made with whole wheat and/or rye flour, which create a somewhat chewy texture and a delectable end result. If you're looking for a hearty style of bread for your grilled cheese sandwich, this is the one.

- If you can't find *pain au levain*, choose sourdough or rye without caraway seeds.

Chapter 1

just cheese

Spinach, Egg, and Manchego

One night I looked in my fridge, saw that I had some spinach, eggs, and of course cheese, and I knew I had to try to create a grilled cheese sandwich with these ingredients. What I didn't know was what a sublime sandwich it would be nor what a great brunch option it is. The only tricky part is getting the egg in the hole, but with a little practice you'll be able to get a hole in one in no time.

- -

3 tablespoons plus 1 teaspoon butter, divided, at room temperature

½ medium onion, finely chopped

8 ounces baby spinach

Salt and freshly ground black pepper

8 sandwich-size slices sourdough bread (or use *pain au levain*, Italian, or wheat)

8 ounces manchego cheese, coarsely grated (or use young pecorino, Gouda, or Gruyère)

4 large eggs

In a large nonstick skillet, heat 1 tablespoon plus 1 teaspoon butter over medium heat. Add the onion and cook just until soft but not brown, about 5 minutes. Add the spinach, cover, and cook, tossing with tongs occasionally, until wilted but still fairly bright green, 2 to 3 minutes. Add salt and pepper to taste. Transfer to a plate. Wipe out the skillet with a paper towel but do not wash it. Have a small bowl or cup ready.

To assemble: Using the remaining butter, butter one side of each slice of bread and place on your work surface, buttered side down. Using a 1½-inch-diameter biscuit cutter (or grapefruit spoon or knife), cut a 1½-inch hole in the center of each bread slice. Press the cheese evenly onto 4 bread slices around the hole (it may seem like a lot of cheese, but it's actually just the right amount), followed by the spinach mixture. Top with the remaining bread slices, buttered side up.

For stovetop method: Heat a large nonstick skillet over a medium-low heat for 2 minutes. Put the sandwiches into the skillet (in batches if necessary), cover, and cook for 2 to 3 minutes, until the undersides turn golden brown. Turn the sandwiches and, working quickly, separate 1 egg over the small bowl or cup, allowing the egg white to drip into the cup. Pour the yolk into the hole in the bread and then pour the egg white over it. (If the hole has closed up because the cheese has oozed out, just use a spoon to open it back up again before putting the egg in it.) Sprinkle with salt and pepper to taste.

Cover and cook for 2 to 3 minutes, until the undersides are golden brown and the yolks have begun to set (the egg whites won't have cooked through yet). Carefully turn the sandwiches again (some of the egg white may run off since it is still partially uncooked). Cover and cook for 1 to 3 minutes, depending on how you like your eggs. Cut in half diagonally and serve immediately.

NOTE: This sandwich cannot be made in a sandwich maker.

Makes 4 sandwiches

Due Due (Double Cheese Sandwich)

Pronounced DO-ay, *due* is the Italian word for "two." Chef Ryan Hardy of the restaurant Montagna at The Little Nell in Aspen, Colorado, created and named this sublime sandwich after the two cheeses he calls for in the recipe, as well as for the unusual Italian cheese Robiola Due Latte, which is made with both cow's and sheep's milk. While it's fairly widely available, if you can't find robiola, just use Brie. No matter what, you'll love the combination of flavors, especially when you add the sweet-spicy *Mostarda di Mediterranea* (page 144). Note that although Ryan's recipe calls for truffles or truffle paste, it's entirely optional.

- -

4 ciabatta rolls, or 1 ciabatta loaf cut into 4 (3-inch-wide) pieces

2 tablespoons butter, at room temperature

2 tablespoons plus 2 teaspoons Dijon mustard

3 to 4 grams fresh white truffles, shaved, or 1 teaspoon white truffle paste (optional)

8 ounces Robiola Due Latte or Tre Latte cheese, sliced ¼ inch thick (or use Brie)

4 ounces fontina cheese, coarsely grated

Mostarda di Mediterranea, for dipping (page 144)

To assemble: Slice the rolls or bread in half horizontally. Place the bread crust side up and spread with the butter. Turn the bottom (flat) halves of the bread, buttered side down, on your work surface. Spread each piece with 2 teaspoons mustard and the truffles or truffle paste. Lay the Robiola slices on the bread and top with the fontina. Top with the remaining bread pieces, buttered-crust side up.

For stovetop method: Heat a large nonstick skillet over medium-low heat for 2 minutes. Put the sandwiches into the pan, cover, and cook for 6 to 7 minutes, until the undersides are golden brown. Turn the sandwiches, pressing each one very firmly with a spatula to compress the bread and filling. Cover and cook for 5 to 6 minutes, until the other sides are well browned. Remove the cover, turn the sandwiches once more, and press firmly with the spatula once again. Cook for 1 to 2 minutes, until the grated cheese has melted completely. (You may need to peek inside one of the sandwiches to make sure.) Remove from the pan and let cool for 5 minutes. Cut in half and serve with the *mostarda* alongside as a sandwich dip.

For sandwich maker method: Preheat the sandwich maker. Follow directions for assembly above. Cook according to manufacturer's instructions.

Makes 4 sandwiches

Burrata with Roasted Peppers and Arugula

Burrata doesn't translate to "rich and creamy" in English, but it just as well might. This seductive cheese, originally from southern Italy, is essentially a ball-shaped pouch made of a thin "skin" of mozzarella stretched around a mixture of cream and strips of mozzarella. You can find it in specialty foods stores and cheese shops around the country. If you can't find it, use fresh mozzarella instead.

- -

3 tablespoons olive oil

8 sandwich-size slices Italian bread (or use sourdough or French)

1 (8-ounce) piece burrata, quartered (or use water-packed mozzarella, sliced ¼ inch thick)

4 ounces roasted red peppers from a jar, drained (or make your own)

1¼ cups packed arugula, stems removed

Salt

To assemble: Brush oil on one side of each of the bread slices. Place 4 slices of bread, oil side down, on your work surface. Put the cheese on the bread and spread lightly to distribute evenly. Lay the peppers on top of the cheese. Pile the arugula onto the peppers. Use your hands to compress lightly if necessary. Drizzle with 1 tablespoon olive oil, and sprinkle with a little salt to taste. Top with the remaining bread slices, oil side up.

For stovetop method: Heat a large nonstick skillet over medium heat for 2 minutes. Put the sandwiches into the pan, cover, and cook for 3 to 4 minutes, until the undersides are well browned. Turn the sandwiches, pressing each one *lightly* with a spatula to flatten slightly (you don't want the burrata to come spurting out). Cover and cook for 2 to 3 minutes, until the second side is golden brown. Turn the sandwiches once more, press firmly with the spatula, cook for 1 minute, and remove from the pan. Let cool for 5 minutes. Cut in half and serve.

For sandwich maker method: Preheat the sandwich maker. Follow directions for assembly above. Cook according to manufacturer's instructions.

NOTE: Depending on the weight of your sandwich maker lid, the creamy cheese might end up oozing out the sides of the sandwich. For this reason, I'd experiment with one sandwich first. If the cheese doesn't ooze, then go ahead and make the others. Otherwise, follow the stovetop method.

Makes 4 sandwiches

Double Cheddar and Tomato Jam

It seems that almost everybody likes the combination of grilled cheese and tomato soup. The easy-to-make Tomato Jam (page 148) is a variation on that theme, because the rich tomato flavor that's usually in the soup goes directly into the sandwich. The double cheddar is your cue that not only is there cheese on the inside of the sandwich, but it's also on the outside. The result is a little sweet, a little savory, a little crunchy, a little salty, and a lot enjoyable.

- -

12 ounces cheddar cheese

4 tablespoons butter, at room temperature

8 sandwich-size slices sourdough bread

6 tablespoons Tomato Jam (page 148)

Using the very small holes of a box grater or other similar-size grating device, finely grate 6 ounces of the cheddar. Place the cheese in a small bowl. Add the butter and, using the back of a fork, mash the mixture until the cheese is well incorporated into the butter.

Using the large holes of a box grater or other similar-size grating device, grate the remaining cheese.

To assemble: Spread the cheddar-butter mixture on one side of each of the bread slices. Place 4 slices of bread, buttered side down, on your work surface. Spread 1½ tablespoons of jam on each slice. Distribute the cheese, and top with the remaining bread slices, buttered side up.

For stovetop method: Heat a large nonstick skillet over medium heat for 2 minutes. Put the sandwiches into the pan, cover, and cook for 3 to 4 minutes, until golden brown. Turn the sandwiches, pressing each one firmly with a spatula to flatten slightly. Cover and cook for 2 to 3 minutes, until the undersides are well browned (watch carefully because the cheese on the outside of the bread can darken quickly). Turn the sandwiches once more, press firmly with the spatula again, cook for 1 minute, and remove from the pan. Let cool for 5 minutes. Cut in half and serve.

For sandwich maker method: Preheat the sandwich maker. Follow directions for assembly above. Cook according to manufacturer's instructions.

Makes 4 sandwiches

Spicy, Crunchy, Sweet Goat Cheese Melt

Creamy goat cheese and tangy dried apricots together create amazing flavors and textures. The surprise element here is the peppercorns, which add an unexpected zing. When put between slices of crunchy walnut bread, this is as much an elegant hors d'oeuvre as it is a humble grilled cheese sandwich. Just cut each sandwich into small squares, place them on a platter, and serve.

1 tablespoon green peppercorns (dry, not brined; or use black peppercorns)

8 ounces goat cheese, at room temperature

1 tablespoon plus 1 teaspoon milk, plus more if needed

2 ounces dried apricots, finely chopped

2 teaspoons honey

1 teaspoon finely chopped fresh thyme

8 sandwich-size slices walnut bread (or use multigrain or olive bread)

2 tablespoons olive oil

Place the peppercorns in a sturdy plastic bag and use the side of a cleaver, a meat mallet, or a heavy can to crack the peppercorns. You don't want to crush them into a powder; you just want them to crack into smaller coarse pieces.

In a small bowl, mix together the goat cheese and milk until smooth and creamy. If the mixture is quite stiff, add more milk 1 teaspoon at a time. Add the apricots, honey, peppercorns, and thyme and stir until well mixed.

To assemble: Brush one side of each of the bread slices with the oil. Place 4 slices of bread, oil side down, on your work surface. Divide and spread the goat cheese mixture on the bread. Top with the remaining bread slices, oil side up.

For stovetop method: Heat a large nonstick skillet over medium heat for 2 minutes. Put the sandwiches into the pan, cover, and cook for 3 to 4 minutes, until golden brown. Turn the sandwiches, pressing each one lightly with a spatula to flatten slightly. Cover and cook for 3 to 4 minutes, until the undersides are golden brown. Turn the sandwiches once more and cook for about 1 minute, or until the filling appears to be heated through. Remove from the pan and let cool for 5 minutes. Cut in half and serve.

For sandwich maker method: Preheat the sandwich maker. Follow directions for assembly above. Cook according to manufacturer's instructions.

Makes 4 sandwiches

Provençal-Style Grilled Cheese

This sandwich's simplicity belies its sophistication. The herbes de Provence in the bread give it an earthy flair, and the tomato provides a zesty counterpoint to both the herbs and the gooey cheese.

8 ounces Monterey Jack cheese, coarsely grated

2 teaspoons herbes de Provence (or use a combination of equal parts dried thyme, lavender, fennel seed, and dried basil)

2 tablespoons butter, at room temperature

8 sandwich-size slices *pain au levain* (or use sourdough bread)

1 large tomato, cut into 8 (¼-inch-thick) slices

Salt

In a small bowl, mix together the cheese and the herbs.

To assemble: Spread butter on one side of each of the bread slices. Place 4 slices of bread, buttered side down, on your work surface. Place half the cheese mixture on the bread slices, followed by the tomatoes. Lightly salt the tomatoes and top with the remaining cheese. Top with the remaining bread slices, buttered side up.

For stovetop method: Heat a large nonstick skillet over medium heat for 2 minutes. Put the sandwiches into the pan, cover, and cook for 2 to 3 minutes, until golden brown. Turn the sandwiches, pressing each one firmly with a spatula to flatten slightly. Cover and cook for 2 to 3 minutes, until the undersides are well browned. Turn the sandwiches once more, press firmly with the spatula again, cook for 1 minute, and remove from the pan. Let cool for 5 minutes. Cut in half and serve.

For sandwich maker method: Preheat the sandwich maker. Follow directions for assembly above. Cook according to manufacturer's instructions.

Makes 4 sandwiches

Hog Island Grilled Cheese

This sandwich is a favorite among San Franciscans. Never mind that it comes to hungry diners by way of an oyster bar. At Hog Island Oyster Bar, people line up for oysters as well as for this sandwich, the restaurant's one concession to the fruits of the land. There, they use a northern California cheese called St. George, but because that's not widely available I've substituted cheddar and Havarti, which together taste very similar to St. George. A word of caution: Keep plenty of napkins on hand for this!

- -

2 tablespoons butter, at room temperature

8 sandwich-size slices *pain au levain* (or use sourdough bread)

4 ounces *fromage blanc*

4 ounces Gruyère cheese, coarsely grated (or use Comté or Swiss)

4 ounces cheddar cheese, coarsely grated

4 ounces Havarti cheese, coarsely grated

To assemble: Butter one side of each slice of bread. Place 4 slices, buttered side down, on your work surface. Spread the *fromage blanc* on each slice. Layer with the Gruyère, cheddar, and Havarti cheeses. You may need to use your hand to compress the cheese. Top with the remaining bread slices, buttered side up.

For stovetop method: Heat a large nonstick skillet over medium heat for 2 minutes. Put the sandwiches into the pan, cover, and cook for 3 to 5 minutes, until the undersides are golden brown. Turn the sandwiches, pressing each one firmly with a spatula to flatten slightly. Cover and cook for 3 to 4 minutes, until the undersides are well browned. Remove the cover, turn the sandwiches once more, and press firmly with the spatula once again. Cook for 1 minute, or until the cheese has melted completely.

(You may need to peek inside to make sure.) Remove from the pan and let cool for 5 minutes. Cut in half and serve.

For sandwich maker method: Preheat the sandwich maker. Follow directions for assembly above. Cook according to manufacturer's instructions.

Makes 4 sandwiches

Chapter 2

meat and cheese

Classic with a Twist

As you'll see, the onions in this sandwich are not cooked. Soaking them in cold water minimizes their pungency and sets them up for a crisp and clean contrast to the rich cheese and salty bacon. I'm hoping you'll like how they taste so much that you'll be tempted to use the onions in other sandwiches too.

- -

½ small red onion (about 4 ounces), very thinly sliced

8 slices bacon

2 tablespoons butter, at room temperature

8 sandwich-size slices sourdough bread

8 ounces cheddar cheese, coarsely grated

8 (¼-inch-thick) center-cut tomato slices (from 1 large or 2 medium tomatoes)

Salt

Fill a medium bowl with very cold water. Place the onion slices in the water and let sit for at least 15 minutes and up to 1 hour. Drain and pat dry. Set aside.

Line a plate with paper towels. Cook the bacon in a large nonstick skillet over medium heat until crisp. Drain on the paper towels. Wipe out the skillet with a paper towel but do not wash it.

To assemble: Spread the butter on one side of each of the bread slices. Place 4 slices of bread, buttered side down, on your work surface. Distribute the onions over the bread, followed by half of the cheese and the tomato slices. Sprinkle the tomatoes with a little salt. Put the remaining cheese on top of the tomatoes and follow with 2 strips of bacon per bread slice. (Depending on the size of your bread, you may only be able to fit one slice of bacon on your sandwich. In that case, break it in half crosswise so that it covers most of the sandwich.) Top with the remaining bread slices, buttered side up.

For stovetop method: Heat a large nonstick skillet over medium heat for 2 minutes. Put the sandwiches into the pan, cover, and cook for 3 to 4 minutes, until golden brown. Turn the sandwiches, pressing each one firmly with a spatula to flatten slightly. Cover and cook for 2 to 3 minutes, until the undersides are golden brown. Remove the cover and turn the sandwiches once more. Press firmly with the spatula again, cook for 1 minute, and remove from the pan. Let cool for 5 minutes. Cut in half and serve.

For sandwich maker method: Preheat the sandwich maker. Follow directions for assembly above. Cook according to manufacturer's instructions.

Makes 4 sandwiches

Mozzarella with Crispy Prosciutto and Broccoli Rabe

Broccoli rabe, also known as rapini, is a bitter green often used in Italian cooking. When nestled in the folds of the gooey mozzarella, the greens along with the crispy prosciutto create a sandwich almost as soulful as Italy itself.

- -

8 thin slices prosciutto (about 4 ounces)

¼ cup olive oil

12 ounces broccoli rabe (about 1 bunch), tough stems removed and coarsely chopped (or use Swiss chard or Tuscan kale)

1 teaspoon freshly squeezed lemon juice

⅛ teaspoon red pepper flakes

⅛ teaspoon salt

8 sandwich-size slices Italian bread (or use *pain au levain* or sourdough)

8 ounces mozzarella cheese, drained and sliced if water-packed; otherwise coarsely grated

Heat a large nonstick skillet over medium heat and line a plate with paper towels. Add the prosciutto slices to the skillet (you may need to do this in batches) and cook until browned and crisp, about 2 minutes on each side. Transfer to the paper towels to drain. The prosciutto will become crisper as it cools.

Add enough oil to make 2 tablespoons fat in the pan. Heat over medium-high heat for 1 minute. Add the broccoli rabe. Cook, stirring occasionally, until soft, tender, and bright green yet caramelized around a few of the edges, 5 to 7 minutes. (Add water to the pan if it seems dry.) Add the lemon juice, red pepper flakes, and salt and toss to coat. Transfer the broccoli rabe to a plate. Wipe out the skillet but don't wash it.

To assemble: Brush the remaining oil on one side of each slice of bread. Place 4 slices of bread, oil side down, on your work surface. Distribute the broccoli rabe and follow with the prosciutto. Pile the cheese on top, compressing it with your hand if necessary, and top with the remaining bread slices, oil side up.

For stovetop method: Heat a large nonstick skillet over medium heat for 2 minutes. Put the sandwiches into the pan, cover, and cook for 3 to 4 minutes, until the undersides are golden brown. Turn the sandwiches, pressing each one firmly with a spatula to flatten slightly. Cover and cook for 2 to 3 minutes, until the undersides are well browned. Remove the cover, turn the sandwiches once more, and press firmly with the spatula once again. Cook for 1 minute, or until the cheese has melted completely. Remove from the pan and let cool for 5 minutes. Cut in half and serve.

For sandwich maker method: Preheat the sandwich maker. Follow directions for assembly above. Cook according to manufacturer's instructions.

Makes 4 sandwiches

Sweet-Tart
Cheddar and Chorizo

This cheesy, crusty sausage-filled sandwich has two special ingredients: cocktail onions and dates. Cookbook author extraordinaire Sheri Castle suggested the latter because of her affection for the sausage-stuffed dates often found at Spanish tapas bars. I wholeheartedly agree.

. . . .

8 ounces Mexican-style fresh chorizo sausage (not Spanish-style)

⅔ cup cocktail onions, drained and coarsely chopped

8 dried dates, pitted and coarsely chopped

4 large ciabatta rolls (about 5 by 3 inches), or 1 large ciabatta loaf cut into 3-inch-wide pieces

2 tablespoons olive oil

8 ounces cheddar cheese, coarsely grated

2 small tart-sweet apples (such as Pink Lady or Braeburn), cut into 16 (¼-inch) slices

If your chorizo is link-style, remove the casings. Line a bowl with paper towels. Crumble the chorizo and cook in a large nonstick skillet over medium-high heat until the meat is uniformly brown. You don't want any raw pieces. Drain in the prepared bowl. Remove any fat from the pan and wipe the pan clean with a paper towel, but do not wash it.

Once the chorizo has cooled slightly, remove the paper towel from the bowl. Add the onions and dates and mix thoroughly.

To assemble: Cut the rolls or bread in half horizontally. Pinch out some of the soft center from the middle of each roll or piece of bread to create a well. Place the bread, crust side up, on your work surface. Brush each piece of bread with olive oil. Place 4 pieces of bread, oil side down, on your work surface. Distribute the chorizo mixture over these bread slices, followed by the cheese and the apple slices. Top with the remaining bread pieces, oil side up.

For stovetop method: Heat a large nonstick skillet over medium-low heat for 2 minutes. Put the sandwiches into the pan, cover, and cook for 4 to 6 minutes, until the undersides are well browned. Carefully turn the sandwiches, pressing each one very firmly with a spatula to compress the filling. (This can be a little more difficult with ciabatta because it's such a hearty bread. Just do the best you can.) Cover and cook for 4 to 5 minutes, until the undersides are golden brown. Turn the sandwiches once more, press firmly with the spatula again, and cook for 1 to 2 minutes, until the sandwiches are heated through and the cheese has melted completely. (You might need to peek inside one of the sandwiches to make sure.) Let cool for 5 minutes. Cut in half and serve.

For sandwich maker method: Preheat the sandwich maker. Follow directions for assembly above. Cook according to manufacturer's instructions.

Makes 4 sandwiches

Say *Oui* to Normandy

Camembert originally comes from the Normandy region of France, which is also well known for its apples. This sandwich brings the two regional specialties together along with ham, which adds a delicious salty-smoky element to the sweet-tart apples and molten cheese.

- -

2 tablespoons butter, at room temperature

8 sandwich-size slices *pain au levain* (or use sourdough or Italian bread)

8 ounces Camembert cheese, sliced ¼ inch thick (or use Brie)

1 teaspoon finely chopped fresh thyme

4 (1-ounce) slices Black Forest ham

1 large tart green apple (such as Granny Smith or Pippin), cut into 16 very thin slices

To assemble: Spread butter on one side of each of the bread slices. Place 4 slices of bread, buttered side down, on your work surface. Place the cheese on the bread. Sprinkle with the thyme. Follow with the ham and apple slices. Top with the remaining bread slices, buttered side up.

For stovetop method: Heat a large nonstick skillet over medium heat for 2 minutes. Put the sandwiches into the pan, cover, and cook for 2 to 3 minutes, until well browned. Turn the sandwiches, pressing each one lightly with a spatula to flatten slightly. Cover and cook for 2 to 3 minutes, until the undersides are golden brown. Turn the sandwiches once more, cook for 1 minute, and remove from the pan. Let cool for 5 minutes. Cut in half and serve.

For sandwich maker method: Preheat the sandwich maker. Follow directions for assembly above. Cook according to manufacturer's instructions.

Makes 4 sandwiches

Sweet and Spicy Chicken and Gouda

The easy-to-make caraway mustard sauce really lends an exotic flavor to this sandwich, especially with the addition of the golden raisins. It all comes together with the sautéed chicken, which soaks up the sauce and plays host to the gobs of melted Gouda, creating memorable flavors and textures.

- -

2 tablespoons Dijon mustard

4 teaspoons mayonnaise

1 teaspoon caraway seed

½ cup golden raisins

2 (8-ounce) boneless, skinless chicken breasts, halved crosswise and pounded to about ½ inch thick

¼ cup plus 1 tablespoon olive oil

¾ teaspoon salt

½ teaspoon garlic powder

½ teaspoon freshly ground black pepper

1 medium onion, halved lengthwise and sliced into ¼-inch-thick strips

4 ciabatta rolls, or 1 ciabatta loaf cut into 4 (3-inch-wide) pieces

8 ounces Gouda cheese, coarsely grated (or use Havarti, Monterey Jack, or Swiss)

To make the sauce: In a small bowl, mix together the mustard, mayonnaise, and caraway seed. Set aside. (You can make the sauce up to 1 day ahead. Cover and refrigerate until ready to use.)

Place the raisins in a small bowl. Cover with very hot or boiling water and let sit for 15 minutes. Drain well and set aside.

To make the chicken: Brush both sides of the chicken with 2 tablespoons of the oil. Sprinkle with salt, garlic powder, and pepper. Put the chicken in a large nonstick skillet and cook over medium heat until the undersides are light brown, 5 to 7 minutes. Turn and cook for about 6 more minutes, or until the chicken is golden brown and firm but not hard. To test for doneness, insert the tip of a knife. The juices should run yellow, not pink. Transfer the chicken to a plate. Wipe out the skillet with a paper towel but do not wash it.

Heat 1 tablespoon of the oil in the skillet over medium heat. Add the onion and cook, stirring occasionally, until golden brown and slightly charred on the edges, 7 to 9 minutes. Add the raisins and cook just until heated through. Sprinkle with salt and pepper to taste. Transfer to a plate. Wipe out the skillet with a paper towel but do not wash it.

To assemble: Cut the ciabatta in half horizontally. Place the bread, crust side up, on your work surface and brush with the remaining 2 tablespoons oil. Turn 4 slices of bread, oil side down, on your work surface. Spread those bread pieces with the mustard sauce and follow with the onion mixture. Place a chicken breast on the onions and distribute the cheese on top of the chicken. Use your hands to compress the cheese if necessary. Top with the remaining bread pieces, cut side down.

For stovetop method: Heat a large nonstick skillet over medium-low heat for 2 minutes. Put the sandwiches into the pan, cover, and cook for 6 to 7 minutes, until the undersides are golden brown. Turn the sandwiches, pressing each one very firmly with a spatula to compress the bread and filling. Cover and cook for 5 to 6 minutes, until the undersides are well browned. Remove the cover, turn the sandwiches once more, and press firmly with the spatula once again. Cook for 1 minute, or until the cheese has melted completely. (You may need to peek inside one of the sandwiches to make sure.) Remove from the pan and let cool for 5 minutes. Cut in half and serve.

For sandwich maker method: Preheat the sandwich maker. Follow directions for assembly above. Cook according to manufacturer's instructions.

Makes 4 sandwiches

Italian Melt

No question, this sandwich is rich. But isn't that what the best grilled cheese sandwiches are supposed to be? It isn't one-dimensional, though. The addition of orange zest to the butter, along with the crunchy fennel, provides refreshing flavors and a welcome textural contrast to the creamy fontina, crispy pancetta, and salty blue cheese.

- ½ fennel bulb (about 8 ounces), cored and sliced about ⅛ inch thick
- ¼ cup water
- 3 tablespoons white wine vinegar
- 4 (1½-ounce) slices pancetta
- 2 tablespoons butter, at room temperature
- 2 teaspoons grated orange zest
- 8 sandwich-size slices Italian bread
- 6 ounces creamy Gorgonzola cheese (such as Gorgonzola Dolce), at room temperature
- 8 ounces fontina cheese, coarsely grated

Place the fennel, water, and vinegar in a small bowl. Let sit for at least 15 minutes or up to 24 hours, refrigerated.

Meanwhile, line a plate with paper towels. In a large nonstick skillet, cook the pancetta over medium-high heat, turning occasionally, until lightly browned and crisp, about 5 minutes. Transfer the pancetta to the paper towels to drain. Wipe out the skillet with a paper towel but do not wash it. Set aside.

In a small bowl, mix together the butter with the orange zest until the zest is thoroughly incorporated.

To assemble: Spread the orange butter on one side of each of the bread slices. Place 4 slices of bread, buttered side down, on your work surface. Spread the Gorgonzola on the bread. Follow with the pancetta slices. Drain the fennel, pat dry, and place on top of the pancetta. Distribute the fontina and top with the remaining bread slices, buttered side up.

For stovetop method: Heat a large nonstick skillet over medium heat for 2 minutes. Put the sandwiches into the pan, cover, and cook for 3 to 4 minutes, until golden brown. Turn the sandwiches, pressing each one firmly with a spatula to help compress the filling. Cover and cook for 3 to 4 minutes, until the undersides are well browned. Turn the sandwiches once more, press with the spatula, and cook for 1 minute. Remove from the pan. Let cool for 5 minutes. Cut in half and serve.

For sandwich maker method: Preheat the sandwich maker. Follow directions for assembly above. Cook according to manufacturer's instructions.

Makes 4 sandwiches

Smoky Kim-Cheese

Every so often, a food or ingredient becomes the "it" food. Right now, that food seems to be kim chee from Korea. The fermented spicy cabbage-and-garlic mixture (think very flavorful sauerkraut) is full of flavor and, as I discovered, goes very well with smoked foods, including smoked cheese. You can find kim chee in the refrigerated section of many grocery and gourmet foods stores.

- -

    4 mini baguettes or sub rolls (or cut 1 baguette into 4 equal-size pieces)
    3 tablespoons olive oil
    ½ cup kim chee
    8 ounces smoked Gouda, coarsely grated
    4 (1-ounce) slices ham, such as Black Forest

To assemble: Cut the bread in half horizontally. Pinch out some of the soft center from the middle of the bread to create a well. Place the bread, crust side up, and brush with the oil. Place 4 pieces of bread, oil side down, on your work surface. Tuck the kim chee into the well of the bread. Distribute the cheese and fold the ham slices over the cheese. Top with the remaining bread, crust side up.

For stovetop method: Heat a large nonstick skillet over medium-low heat for 3 minutes. Put the sandwiches into the pan, cover, and cook for 5 to 6 minutes, until evenly browned. Remove the cover and turn the sandwiches, pressing each one very firmly with a spatula to help compress the filling and bread. Cover and cook for 4 to 5 minutes, until the undersides are well browned. Turn the sandwiches once more, press firmly with the spatula again, cook for 1 to 2 minutes, until the bread is well browned and the cheese has melted completely. (You may need to peek inside to make sure.) Remove from the pan and let cool for 5 minutes.

For sandwich maker method: Preheat the sandwich maker. Follow directions for assembly above. Cook according to manufacturer's instructions.

Makes 4 sandwiches

French Mountain Glory

This sandwich gives a nod to the ingredients that compose a French mountain dish called *tartiflette*. The two stars of the dish are an exquisite cave-aged French mountain cheese called Comté and a rather strong cheese called Reblochon. Don't worry if you don't like strong cheeses, though. Brie or Camembert make fine substitutions. Bacon and onions round out the traditional dish, and usually potatoes do too. But here, the potatoes are part of the bread.

- -

4 slices bacon

½ medium onion (about 4 ounces), thinly sliced

Salt

8 ounces Comté cheese, coarsely grated (or use Gruyère, raclette, or Swiss)

8 cornichons, coarsely chopped (or use 2 medium dill pickles)

2 tablespoons butter, at room temperature

8 sandwich-size slices potato bread (or use country white or French)

6 ounces Reblochon cheese, sliced (or use Pont l'Évêque, Camembert, or Brie)

Line a plate with paper towels. Cook the bacon in a large nonstick skillet over medium-high heat until crisp. Transfer the bacon to the paper towels to drain. When cool, break each slice in half. Set aside.

Discard all but about 1 tablespoon bacon fat from the skillet. Add the onion and cook over medium heat until soft and beginning to brown around the edges, 8 to 10 minutes. Salt lightly.

In a small bowl, toss the Comté and cornichons together.

To assemble: Spread butter on one side of each slice of bread. Place 4 slices of bread, buttered side down, on your work surface. Distribute the onion on the bread, followed by the Comté-cornichon mixture and the Reblochon. Place the bacon slices on the cheese and top with the remaining bread slices, buttered side up.

For stovetop method: Heat a large nonstick skillet over medium heat for 2 minutes. Put the sandwiches into the pan, cover, and cook for 3 to 4 minutes, until the undersides are golden brown. Turn the sandwiches, pressing each one firmly with a spatula to compress the filling. Cover and cook for 3 to 4 minutes, until the undersides are well browned. Turn the sandwiches once more, press firmly with the spatula again, cook for 1 minute, and remove from the pan. Let cool for 5 minutes. Cut in half and serve.

For sandwich maker method: Preheat the sandwich maker. Follow directions for assembly above. Cook according to manufacturer's instructions.

Makes 4 sandwiches

Chapter 3

anything goes

Cheese and Cherries
à la Lynne

One of the best cooks and gardeners I know, my friend Lynne Devereux is also a devoted cheese person. She is a particularly big fan of *fromage blanc*. The somewhat tart ricotta-like cheese has a luscious texture and is wonderfully versatile. When Lynne gave me two beautiful lemons from her tree and happened to mention her love of olive bread, I decided to create a recipe just for her using these and a few other ingredients. The basil and cherries represent the essence of an early summer garden, where I know she loves to spend time, and they add a lovely sweet and herby quality to the creamy sandwich.

¼ cup *fromage blanc* (or use ricotta or fresh goat cheese)

¼ cup finely chopped basil

1 teaspoon finely grated lemon zest

1 cup cherries, pitted and thinly sliced (or use ½ cup dried, soaked in hot water for 15 minutes)

2 tablespoons butter, at room temperature

8 sandwich-size slices olive bread (or use egg, multigrain, or walnut bread)

8 ounces Gruyère cheese, coarsely grated (or use Comté, Emmentaler, or Swiss)

In a small bowl, mix together the *fromage blanc*, basil, lemon zest, and cherries.

To assemble: Spread butter on one side of each of the bread slices. Place 4 slices of bread, buttered side down, on your work surface. Spread the *fromage blanc* mixture on the bread. Follow with the Gruyère. Top with the remaining bread slices, buttered side up.

For stovetop method: Heat a large nonstick skillet over medium heat for 2 minutes. Put the sandwiches into the pan, cover, and cook for 3 to 4 minutes, until well browned. Turn the sandwiches, pressing each one firmly with a spatula to compress the filling slightly. Cover and cook for 2 to 3 minutes, until the undersides are golden brown. Turn the sandwiches once more, press firmly with the spatula again, cook for 1 minute, and remove from the pan. Let cool for 5 minutes. Cut in half and serve.

For sandwich maker method: Preheat the sandwich maker. Follow directions for assembly above. Cook according to manufacturer's instructions.

Makes 4 sandwiches

Chips and Guacamole Grilled Cheese

In this recipe, tortilla chips are on the *outside* of the bread to give the sandwich its corn-like flavor and to give you the ability to enjoy all the flavors—guacamole, bacon, cheeses, and corn chips—all at once.

· ·

8 slices bacon

8 large tortilla chips (about 2 ounces)

4 tablespoons butter, at room temperature

8 slices sourdough bread

½ cup guacamole (recipe follows; or use purchased, preferably one with tomato in it)

2 tablespoons peeled, seeded, diced Roma tomato (see Note)

4 ounces Colby cheese, coarsely grated

4 ounces Monterey Jack cheese, coarsely grated

4 ounces goat cheese

Line a plate with paper towels. In a large nonstick skillet, cook the bacon over medium heat until very crisp. Drain the bacon on the paper towels. Remove the bacon fat from the pan and wipe the pan with a paper towel, but do not wash it. Set aside.

To make the tortilla chip butter, put the chips in the bowl of a food processor and process until the texture is very fine, similar to sand. Alternatively, place the chips in a sturdy plastic bag. Using a meat mallet or other heavy object, pound the chips until they are the texture of sand.

Put the butter in a medium bowl and add the ground chips. Using a fork, work the chip "sand" and butter together until well mixed. The mixture will be somewhat stiff.

To assemble: Spread the butter mixture on one side of each slice of bread. Place 4 slices, butter-chip mixture side down, on your work surface. Spread 2 tablespoons of the guacamole on each slice of bread. Sprinkle the tomato on top of the guacamole. Follow with the colby and Monterey Jack cheeses. Dot with small pieces of the goat cheese. Finish by placing 2 bacon pieces on each sandwich. Top with the remaining bread slices, buttered side up.

For stovetop method: Heat a large nonstick skillet over medium heat for 2 minutes. Put the sandwiches into the pan, cover, and cook for 3 to 4 minutes, until the undersides are golden brown. Watch carefully because the chips in the butter can burn easily. Turn the sandwiches, pressing each one firmly with a spatula to compress the filling slightly. Cover and cook for 2 to 3 minutes, until the undersides are well browned. Turn the sandwiches once more, press firmly with the spatula again, cook for 1 minute, and remove from the pan. Let cool for 5 minutes. Cut in half and serve.

For sandwich maker method: Use your sandwich maker for this sandwich only if it has variable heat settings. Otherwise, it will cook too hot and burn the chips on the bread without melting the cheese. To use your sandwich maker, follow directions for assembly above. Cook according to manufacturer's instructions.

NOTE: There's no need to use the tomato if your guacamole already has tomato in it.

Makes 4 sandwiches

Guacamole

Chef Deborah Schneider has spent a lot of time south of the border in Baja, Mexico. She now brings her Mexican cooking experience north to her Orange County restaurant, SOL Cocina. I adapted her guacamole recipe because of its lovely balance of flavors, which is often tricky to achieve when it comes to making this quintessential avocado dip.

> 1 ripe Hass avocado
> 1 tablespoon freshly squeezed lime juice (from about 1 lime)
> ¼ teaspoon kosher salt
> 2 tablespoons finely diced white onion
> 2 tablespoons finely chopped fresh cilantro
> ½ fresh serrano chile, minced (optional)
> 1 tablespoon cored, seeded, and diced Roma tomato

Split and pit the avocado, and mash the avocado flesh in a medium bowl with the lime juice and salt, using a potato masher or a fork. Do not use a blender or food processor. You want to keep the avocado slightly chunky, not make it soupy. Stir in the onion, cilantro, chile, and tomato. Let sit for about 15 minutes to allow the flavors to meld.

NOTE: This makes more than you need for the sandwiches. Serve the remaining guacamole with chips alongside.

Makes about 1 cup

Crab-Swiss Melt with Asparagus

One of my favorite hors d'oeuvres as a kid was my mom's Swiss-crab melts. She mixed together Swiss cheese, crabmeat, and mayonnaise, put the mixture on crackers, and baked them until they were golden and bubbly. This sandwich pretty much re-creates those flavors, and with apologies to my mother, I might even like this version better.

■ ■

16 thin asparagus spears
Olive oil
Salt
¼ cup mayonnaise
4 ounces lump crabmeat
4 ounces goat cheese
2 tablespoons finely chopped fresh tarragon
2 tablespoons finely chopped fresh chives
½ teaspoon lightly packed lemon zest
Freshly ground black pepper
8 sandwich-size slices Italian bread (or use French or sourdough)
6 ounces Swiss or Emmentaler cheese, coarsely grated

Preheat the oven to 350°F.

Place the asparagus in a shallow baking pan, drizzle with a little olive oil, and sprinkle with salt. Bake for about 7 minutes, or until tender but still firm. When cool enough to handle, cut off the tips and reserve. Cut the stalks into ¼-inch pieces.

In a medium bowl, mix together 2 tablespoons of the mayonnaise, the crabmeat, goat cheese, asparagus pieces, tarragon, chives, and lemon zest. Add a little salt and pepper to taste.

To assemble: Spread the remaining 2 tablespoons mayonnaise on each slice of bread. Place 4 slices, mayonnaise side down, on your work surface. Spread the crab-asparagus mixture on the bread. Follow with the cheese. Lay the asparagus tips on top of the cheese. Top with the remaining bread, mayonnaise side up.

For stovetop method: Heat a large nonstick skillet over medium heat for 2 minutes. Put the sandwiches into the pan, cover, and cook for 3 to 4 minutes, until golden brown. Turn the sandwiches, pressing each one firmly with a spatula to compress the filling slightly. Cover and cook for 2 to 3 minutes, until the undersides are well browned. Turn the sandwiches once more, press firmly with the spatula again, cook for 1 minute, and remove from the pan. Let cool for 5 minutes. Cut in half and serve.

For sandwich maker method: Do not make this sandwich on a sandwich maker unless you can control the weight of the lid. If it's too heavy, the filling is likely to be squeezed out the sides, leaving you with a mess and an empty sandwich.

Makes 4 sandwiches

Brie, Mozzarella, and Pears with Blue Cheese Butter

If you don't like rich sandwiches, then skip this recipe. This sandwich unquestionably falls into the decadent category, but it also falls under the heading of absolutely delicious. The pear-thyme mixture saves the sandwich from being cloying and creates a memorable flavor explosion when combined with the creamy Brie, mozzarella, and blue cheese butter.

- -

3 tablespoons butter

½ large yellow onion, halved lengthwise and thinly sliced (about 1½ cups)

1 medium firm pear (such as Bosc), peeled, cored, and cut into ¼-inch cubes (about ¾ cup)

1 tablespoon finely chopped fresh thyme

¼ teaspoon kosher salt

Freshly ground black pepper

3 ounces creamy blue cheese (such as Maytag, Point Reyes Original Blue, or Gorgonzola), at room temperature

8 sandwich-size slices sourdough bread

6 ounces Brie cheese, sliced ¼ inch thick

8 ounces mozzarella cheese, coarsely grated

Heat 1 tablespoon of the butter in a large nonstick skillet over medium heat. Add the onion and cook until limp but not brown, about 5 minutes. Add the pear and thyme and cook just until heated through, 2 to 3 minutes. Add the salt and pepper. Set aside.

In a small bowl, combine the blue cheese with the remaining 2 tablespoons butter and mash with a fork until well mixed.

To assemble: Spread the blue cheese butter on one side of each of the bread slices. Place 4 slices of bread, buttered side down, on your work surface. Lay the Brie slices on the bread. Follow with the onion-pear mixture and finish with the mozzarella. Top with the remaining bread slices, buttered side up.

For stovetop method: Heat a large nonstick skillet over medium heat for 2 minutes. Put the sandwiches into the pan, cover, and cook for 3 minutes, or until golden brown. Turn the sandwiches, pressing each one firmly with a spatula to compress the filling slightly. Cover and cook for 2 to 3 minutes, until the undersides are well browned. Turn the sandwiches once more, press firmly with the spatula again, cook for 1 minute, and remove from the pan. Let cool for 5 minutes. Cut in half and serve.

For sandwich maker method: Preheat the sandwich maker. Follow directions for assembly above. Cook according to manufacturer's instructions.

Makes 4 sandwiches

Creamy, Cheesy, and Smoky Croissant

Even though croissants have a flaky texture, they make one of the best breads for grilled cheese sandwiches for one simple reason: butter. All that butter makes for a super-crisp and flavorful crust. Add to that melted cheese, and you have nothing less than a taste of heaven.

- 6 tablespoons mayonnaise
- 2 tablespoons Dijon mustard
- 2 medium cloves garlic, minced
- 1 teaspoon finely chopped fresh rosemary
- Salt
- 4 large croissants, halved lengthwise (see Note)
- ¼ cup oil-packed sun-dried tomatoes, drained and coarsely chopped
- 6 ounces Brie cheese, rind removed
- 6 ounces Swiss cheese, coarsely grated
- 4 (1-ounce) slices smoked turkey

In a small bowl, mix together the mayonnaise, mustard, garlic, and rosemary. Add a little salt to taste. Set aside for up to 30 minutes at room temperature or up to 1 day refrigerated.

To assemble: Place the bottom half of each croissant on your work surface, cut side up. Spread 2 tablespoons of the aioli on each croissant half, followed by the sun-dried tomatoes. Lay the Brie slices on top, followed by the Swiss cheese and turkey slices. Top with the remaining croissant halves, cut side down.

For stovetop method: Heat a large nonstick skillet over medium-low heat for 2 minutes. Put the sandwiches into the pan, cover, and cook for 2 to 3 minutes, until golden brown. Carefully turn the sandwiches, pressing each one with a spatula to compress the bread and filling. Cover and cook for 2 to 3 minutes, until the undersides are golden brown. Turn the sandwiches once more, press with the spatula again, cook for 1 minute, and remove from the pan. Let cool for 5 minutes. Cut in half and serve.

For sandwich maker method: Preheat the sandwich maker. Follow directions for assembly above. Cook according to manufacturer's instructions.

NOTE: The weight of the lid of some sandwich makers might be too heavy for the delicate croissant. You may want to experiment with one sandwich before cooking the rest.

NOTE: If you can only find regular-size croissants, you may end up with filling for more than 4 sandwiches. Also, be aware that because of their high butter content, croissants can burn easily. Watch carefully.

Makes 4 sandwiches

Pizza Grilled Cheese

I don't know why I'd never thought of putting some of my favorite pizza ingredients into sandwich form, but I'm glad I finally did. This sandwich combines two of everyone's favorite foods—pizza and grilled cheese sandwiches—and puts them together in one bite.

. . . .

Note that the pizza sauce is optional. The sauce adds a bit more pizzazz, but the sandwich is delectable either way.

3 tablespoons olive oil

8 ounces white or brown mushrooms, stems removed and sliced ¼ inch thick

Salt

4 ciabatta rolls, or 1 ciabatta loaf cut into 4 (3-inch-wide) pieces (or use Italian bread; see Note)

½ cup pizza sauce (not marinara; optional)

12 ounces fresh mozzarella cheese, thinly sliced (or, if using vacuum-packed mozzarella, coarsely grated)

½ cup sliced black olives

4 ounces pepperoni, sliced paper-thin

2 medium tomatoes (about 8 ounces), sliced ¼ inch thick

1 teaspoon dried oregano

½ teaspoon red pepper flakes

Heat 1 tablespoon of the oil in a large nonstick skillet over medium heat. Add the mushrooms and cook, stirring occasionally, until soft, 5 to 7 minutes. (Add a few drops of water if the pan seems dry.) Sprinkle with a little salt and remove from the skillet. Wipe out the skillet with a paper towel but do not wash it.

To assemble: Cut the ciabatta in half horizontally. Pinch out some of the soft centers from each piece of bread to create a well. Turn the bread slices, crust side up, and brush with the remaining 2 tablespoons olive oil. Place 4 pieces of bread, oil side down, on your work surface. Spread half of the pizza sauce on the bread. Place half of the cheese on the bread, and layer with the mushrooms, olives, and pepperoni, followed by the remaining cheese. Place a few tomato slices on top of the cheese and sprinkle with the oregano, pepper flakes, and salt to taste. Spread the remaining pizza sauce on the remaining bread pieces and place on top of the filling, crust side up.

For stovetop method: Heat a large nonstick skillet over medium-low to medium heat for 2 minutes. Put the sandwiches into the pan, cover, and cook for 5 to 6 minutes, until the undersides of the bread begin to brown. Turn the sandwiches, pressing each one very firmly a couple of times with a spatula to compress the bread and filling. Cover and cook for 4 to 5 minutes, until the undersides are golden brown. Turn the sandwiches once more, press firmly once more with the spatula, and cook for 1 to 2 minutes, until the cheese has melted completely. (You'll have to peek inside one of the sandwiches to see if the cheese has melted.) Remove from the pan and let cool for 5 minutes. Cut in half and serve.

For sandwich maker method: Preheat the sandwich maker. Follow directions for assembly above. Cook according to manufacturer's instructions.

NOTE: If you decide to use Italian bread instead of ciabatta, then the heat should be set to medium and the cooking time should be shortened to 3 to 4 minutes on each side.

Makes 4 sandwiches

Gruyère and Gorgonzola with Hazelnut Butter

Some of the best hazelnuts in the world are grown in the northern part of Italy, in the Piedmont region. Nearby, the region of Lombardy is home to Gorgonzola cheese, and just over the mountains in Switzerland is where they make Gruyère. Like the geography that connects the ingredients, the flavors in this delicious sandwich come together seamlessly.

½ cup hazelnuts, toasted (preferably skinned)

1½ teaspoons vegetable oil

2 tablespoons butter, at room temperature

8 sandwich-size slices Italian bread (or use wheat or French)

6 ounces Gruyère cheese (or use Comté, Emmentaler, or Swiss)

6 ounces Gorgonzola Dolce cheese

4 teaspoons honey (preferably chestnut or acacia)

Put the hazelnuts in the bowl of a food processor and process until the hazelnuts are coarsely chopped. Add the oil and continue to process until the mixture is thick but spreadable, similar to chunky peanut butter.

To assemble: Spread butter on one side of each slice of bread. Place 4 slices of bread, buttered side down, on your work surface. Spread the hazelnut butter on the bread. Distribute the Gruyère over the hazelnut butter. Scatter the Gorgonzola over the Gruyère and drizzle with the honey. Top with the remaining bread slices, buttered side up.

For stovetop method: Heat a large nonstick skillet over medium heat for 2 minutes. Put the sandwiches into the pan, cover, and cook for 2 to 3 minutes, until the undersides are well browned. Turn the sandwiches, pressing each one firmly with a spatula to flatten slightly. Cover and cook for 2 to 3 minutes, until the undersides are golden brown. Remove the cover, turn the sandwiches once more, and press firmly with the spatula once again. Cook for 1 minute, or until the cheese has melted completely. Remove from the pan and let cool for 5 minutes. Cut in half and serve.

For sandwich maker method: Preheat the sandwich maker. Follow directions for assembly above. Cook according to manufacturer's instructions.

Makes 4 sandwiches

Shepherd Sandwich with Ham and Tomato

I call this a shepherd sandwich because all the cheeses in the recipe are made from sheep's milk and come from different countries. I decided to use the different cheeses because some sheep's milk cheeses are nutty, and others are buttery, while others are tangy, and many are all of the above. Don't worry if you can't find all the cheeses. The sandwich is just as good with only one or two.

- 2 ounces aged pecorino cheese (such as Pecorino Romano), very finely grated
- 3 tablespoons butter, at room temperature
- 8 sandwich-size slices hearty Italian or French bread (such as *pain au levain*)
- 4 ounces manchego cheese (not extra-aged), coarsely grated
- 4 ounces Pyrenees-style sheep's milk cheese (such as Petit Basque, Ossau-Iraty, or Vermont Shepherd), coarsely grated
- 4 (1-ounce) slices ham
- 8 (¼-inch-thick) center-cut tomato slices (from 1 large or 2 medium tomatoes)
- Salt

In a small bowl, mash the pecorino and butter together until thoroughly mixed.

To assemble: Spread the pecorino butter on one side of each of the bread slices. Place 4 slices of bread, buttered side down, on your work surface. Distribute half the manchego and half the other sheep's milk cheese over the bread. Lay a piece of ham over the cheeses, followed by the tomatoes. Lightly salt the tomatoes and distribute the rest of the cheese over them. You may need to use your hands to compress the cheese. Top with the remaining bread slices, buttered side up.

For stovetop method: Heat a large nonstick skillet over medium heat for 2 minutes. Put the sandwiches into the pan, cover, and cook for 3 to 4 minutes, until golden brown (watch carefully, as the pecorino butter can burn fairly easily). Turn the sandwiches, pressing each one firmly with a spatula to flatten slightly. Cover and cook for 3 to 4 minutes, until the undersides are golden brown. Turn the sandwiches once more, press firmly with the spatula again, cook for 1 minute, and remove from the pan. Let cool for 5 minutes. Cut in half and serve.

For sandwich maker method: Preheat the sandwich maker. Follow directions for assembly above. Cook according to manufacturer's instructions.

Makes 4 sandwiches

Chapter 4

veggies and cheese

Artichoke Dip Grilled Cheese

As the recipe title suggests, this sandwich is based on the popular artichoke dip, an hors d'oeuvre that seems to go even faster at a party than a wheel of Brie. Putting the cheesy dip into sandwich form seemed like a no-brainer, and doing so with olive oil–spiked focaccia adds a fun and tasty twist. To make the filling properly, be sure to drain the artichokes well. Otherwise, your mixture will be watery and your sandwich will be a mess.

- 2 (6-ounce) jars marinated artichokes, drained and coarsely chopped
- 2 tablespoons mayonnaise
- 1 teaspoon Worcestershire sauce
- ½ teaspoon hot sauce, or to your taste
- ½ teaspoon garlic powder
- 4 scallions (white and tender green parts), finely chopped
- 2 ounces Pecorino Romano cheese, coarsely crumbled (or use Parmigiano-Reggiano)
- 4 (4-inch-square) pieces focaccia, split horizontally (or use 8 slices sourdough or Italian bread)
- 8 ounces fontina cheese, coarsely grated (or use Monterey Jack or Havarti)

In a medium bowl, mix together the artichokes, mayonnaise, Worcestershire sauce, hot sauce, garlic powder, scallions, and Pecorino Romano.

To assemble: Place 4 slices of focaccia on your work surface, cut side up. (If your focaccia is especially thick—more than 3 inches—pinch out a small amount of the soft centers to create a better bread-to-filling ratio.) Spread the artichoke mixture on the bread. Distribute the fontina and top with the remaining focaccia slices, cut side down.

For stovetop method: Heat a large nonstick skillet over medium heat for 2 minutes. Put the sandwiches into the pan, cover, and cook for 3 to 4 minutes, until the undersides are golden brown. (Watch carefully, because the high oil content in focaccia can make the bread turn from golden to blackened quickly.) Turn the sandwiches, pressing each one firmly with a spatula to compress the filling slightly. Cover and cook for 3 to 4 minutes, until the undersides are well browned. Remove the cover, turn the sandwiches once more, and press firmly with the spatula once again. Cook for 1 minute, or until the cheese has melted completely. (You might need to peek inside to make sure.) Remove from the pan and let cool for 5 minutes. Cut in half and serve.

For sandwich maker method: Preheat the sandwich maker. Follow directions for assembly above. Cook according to manufacturer's instructions.

Makes 4 sandwiches

Camembert and Comté
with Mushrooms

When mushrooms and two of the world's best cheeses like these are piled high on a baguette, you get a glorious symphony of earthy, creamy, and buttery flavors. Although this sandwich is sublime with almost any type of mushroom, the easy-to-find white or brown ones taste terrific.

- 4 tablespoons butter, at room temperature
- 1 small shallot, finely chopped (about 2 tablespoons)
- 1 large clove garlic, minced
- 8 ounces white or brown mushrooms, stems removed and sliced ¼ inch thick
- 2 teaspoons sherry vinegar (or use red wine vinegar)
- 2 teaspoons finely chopped fresh thyme
- Salt and freshly ground black pepper
- 1 baguette, cut crosswise into 4 (6-inch-wide) pieces
- 6 ounces Camembert cheese, sliced ¼ inch thick
- 8 ounces Comté cheese, coarsely grated (or use Gruyère, Swiss, or fontina)

Melt 2 tablespoons of the butter in a large nonstick skillet over medium-high heat. Add the shallot and cook just until soft, about 5 minutes. Add the garlic and cook for 1 minute. Add the mushrooms and cook until soft, about 5 minutes. Turn the heat to high and add the vinegar. Cook until almost all of the vinegar has boiled away and the mushrooms have begun to caramelize around the edges, 1 to 2 minutes. Add the thyme and salt and pepper to taste. Stir once or twice and remove from the heat. Transfer the mushrooms to a plate and set aside. Wipe out the skillet with a paper towel but do not wash it.

To assemble: Melt the remaining 2 tablespoons butter in a small pan or in the microwave. Cut each baguette piece in half lengthwise. Pinch out a small amount of the soft center of each piece of bread to create a well. Place the baguette pieces, crust side up, on your work surface and spread with butter. Turn the bottom (flat) pieces, crust side down, on your work surface. Distribute the mushroom mixture on the bread, followed by the Camembert. Top with the Comté. Place the remaining baguette pieces on top, crust side up.

For stovetop method: Heat a large nonstick skillet over medium-low heat for 2 minutes. Put the sandwiches in the pan, cover, and cook for 5 to 6 minutes, until evenly browned. Turn the sandwiches, pressing each one very firmly with a spatula to compress the bread and filling. Cover and cook for 3 to 4 minutes, until the undersides are golden brown and the cheese has melted. Turn the sandwiches once more, press firmly with the spatula again, and cook for 1 minute, or until the cheese has completely melted. (You might need to peek inside to make sure.) Remove from the pan and let cool for 5 minutes. Cut in half and serve.

For sandwich maker method: Preheat the sandwich maker. Follow directions for assembly above. Cook according to manufacturer's instructions.

Makes 4 sandwiches

Havarti with Balsamic-Glazed Carrots

Although the idea of glazed carrots in a grilled cheese sandwich may seem odd, wait until you try them. The balsamic glaze creates just enough tang to counter the sweetness of the carrots and the creaminess of the cheese. The best thing about the carrots is that they make a great side dish to lamb or beef. In fact, if you have either of these meats left over from another meal, add a slice to this sandwich to make a hearty and indulgent treat.

- -

2 teaspoons olive oil

1 large carrot, cut into thin 4-inch-long segments

2 tablespoons balsamic vinegar

Salt and freshly ground black pepper

2 tablespoons butter, at room temperature

8 slices rye bread (or use whole-grain or Italian)

8 ounces Havarti cheese, coarsely grated

To make the carrots: Heat the oil in a large nonstick skillet over medium-high heat. Add the carrots and cook, stirring frequently, until caramelized around the edges, 5 to 7 minutes. Turn the heat to medium-low and add the vinegar and salt and pepper to taste. Cover and cook until soft, about 5 minutes. Transfer to a plate. Wipe out the skillet but do not wash it.

To assemble: Butter one side of each slice of bread. Place 4 slices on your work surface, buttered side down. Place the carrots on the bread. Distribute the cheese over the carrots. Top with the remaining bread slices, buttered side up.

For stovetop method: Heat a large nonstick skillet over medium heat for 2 minutes. Put the sandwiches into the pan, cover, and cook for 3 to 4 minutes, until the undersides are golden brown. Turn the sandwiches, pressing each one firmly with a spatula to flatten slightly. Cover and cook for 3 to 4 minutes, until the undersides are golden brown. Remove the cover, turn the sandwiches once more, and press firmly with the spatula once again. Cook for 1 minute, or until the cheese has melted completely. Remove from the pan and let cool for 5 minutes. Cut in half and serve.

For sandwich maker method: Preheat the sandwich maker. Follow directions for assembly above. Cook according to manufacturer's instructions.

Makes 4 sandwiches

Eggplant Parmesan with Fontina and Tomato Jam

Although she wasn't Italian, my grandmother used to make the best eggplant parmesan this side of Italy. I'm sure I liked it so much because of the exceedingly high ratio of cheese to eggplant. When I decided to turn this childhood favorite into a sandwich, I got more than I bargained for. Not only did I swoon over the flavor, but I also loved the innumerable wonderful memories of my grandmother that it evoked.

- -

1 or 2 globe eggplant (about 2 pounds), peeled, ends cut off, and cut crosswise into 8 (¼-inch-thick) slices

6 tablespoons olive oil

Salt and freshly ground black pepper

2 teaspoons finely chopped fresh oregano (or use ¾ teaspoon dried)

2 ounces parmesan cheese, finely grated

4 (4-inch-square) pieces focaccia (or use Italian bread, sub rolls, or mini baguettes)

6 tablespoons Tomato Jam (page 148)

8 ounces fontina cheese, coarsely grated

Place an oven rack 6 inches below the heating element and preheat the broiler.

To prepare the eggplant: Place the eggplant on a baking sheet and brush with 2 tablespoons of the oil. Sprinkle lightly with salt and pepper. Broil for 5 to 6 minutes, until it begins to brown. Turn the eggplant and brush with another 2 tablespoons of the oil. Sprinkle with the oregano and parmesan.

Broil for 1 to 2 more minutes, until the cheese is golden brown. Watch carefully! Let cool.

To assemble: Cut the focaccia pieces in half horizontally. Brush the remaining 2 tablespoons of oil on one side of each piece of bread. Place 4 pieces of bread, oil side down, on your work surface. Spread the jam on the bread and place a couple of pieces of eggplant on each slice (you may need to cut the eggplant to fit the size of your bread). Distribute the cheese, and top with the remaining focaccia pieces, oil side up.

For stovetop method: Heat a large nonstick skillet over medium-low heat for 2 minutes. Put the sandwiches into the pan, cover, and cook for 3 to 4 minutes, until the undersides are golden brown. Turn the sandwiches, pressing each one firmly with a spatula to compress the filling. Cover and cook for 3 to 4 minutes, until the undersides are well browned. Turn the sandwiches once more, press firmly with the spatula again, and cook for 1 minute, or until the cheese has melted completely. (You might need to peek inside to make sure.) Remove from the pan and let cool for 5 minutes. Cut in half and serve.

For sandwich maker method: Preheat the sandwich maker. Follow directions for assembly above. Cook according to manufacturer's instructions.

Makes 4 sandwiches

Spring Pea Pesto and Fontina

Even though you can make this year-round, there's nothing like the fresh flavor of the first peas of spring to liven the spirit after a long winter. The pea mixture is great on its own, so you might think about making a double batch and saving the extra to put on toasted baguette slices to serve as hors d'oeuvres.

- -

2 cups water

1 teaspoon salt

⅔ cup fresh or frozen peas

¼ cup packed fresh basil leaves, torn

3 tablespoons ricotta cheese

3 tablespoons pine nuts, lightly toasted

1 tablespoon freshly squeezed lemon juice

¼ teaspoon salt, or more to taste

Freshly ground black pepper

1 ounce pecorino cheese, finely grated (or use parmesan)

3 tablespoons butter, at room temperature

8 sandwich-size slices Italian or French bread

8 ounces fontina cheese, coarsely grated (or use mozzarella or Monterey Jack)

In a small saucepan, bring the water and salt to a boil. Add the peas and cook for 3 to 4 minutes, just until tender. Drain and cool.

Put the peas, basil, ricotta, garlic, pine nuts, lemon juice, and salt in the bowl of a food processor. Process until smooth. Taste and add more salt, if necessary, along with a few grinds of pepper.

In a small bowl, mix the pecorino with the butter until the cheese is well incorporated.

To assemble: Spread the butter mixture on one side of each slice of bread. Place 4 slices, buttered side down, on your work surface. Spread about 2 tablespoons pea mixture on the bread. Follow with the fontina. Top with the remaining bread slices, buttered side up.

For stovetop method: Heat a large nonstick skillet over medium heat for 2 minutes. Put the sandwiches into the pan, cover, and cook for 3 to 4 minutes, until the undersides are golden brown. Turn the sandwiches, pressing each one firmly with a spatula to flatten slightly. Cover and cook for 2 to 3 minutes, until the undersides are well browned. Remove the cover, turn the sandwiches once more, and press firmly with the spatula once again. Cook for 1 minute, or until the cheese has melted completely. Remove from the pan and let cool for 5 minutes. Cut in half and serve.

For sandwich maker method: Preheat the sandwich maker. Follow directions for assembly above. Cook according to manufacturer's instructions.

Makes 4 sandwiches

Alpine Grilled Cheese with Pickled Shallots and Watercress

The combination of the world's best melting cheeses, along with pickled shallots and watercress, can't help but bring this sandwich to alpine heights. If you can't find all of the cheeses, just use more of the ones you *can* find to add up to the quantity of cheese called for in the recipe.

- ¼ cup cider vinegar
- ¼ cup water
- 2 tablespoons sugar
- 1 teaspoon salt
- 4 small shallots (about 6 ounces), very thinly sliced
- 2 tablespoons butter, at room temperature
- 8 sandwich-size slices *pain au levain*, sourdough, multigrain, or dark rye bread
- 1⅓ cups lightly packed watercress leaves (about 1 ounce; or use arugula or baby spinach)
- 2 ounces Emmentaler cheese, coarsely grated
- 2 ounces Gruyère cheese, coarsely grated
- 2 ounces Comté cheese, coarsely grated
- 2 ounces Pleasant Ridge Reserve cheese, coarsely grated

Place the vinegar, water, sugar, and salt in a medium bowl. Mix well to dissolve the sugar. Add the shallots and let sit for at least 1 hour and up to 2 days, refrigerated.

To assemble: Butter one side of each slice of bread. Place 4 slices, buttered side down, on your work surface. Drain the shallots and pat dry. Scatter about 2 tablespoons shallot slices on the bread. Follow with the watercress. Distribute the cheeses and top with the remaining bread slices, buttered side up.

For stovetop method: Heat a large nonstick skillet over medium heat for 2 minutes. Put the sandwiches into the pan, cover, and cook for 3 to 4 minutes, until the undersides are golden brown. Turn the sandwiches, pressing each one firmly with a spatula to flatten slightly. Cover and cook for 3 to 4 minutes, until the undersides are well browned. Remove the cover, turn the sandwiches once more, and press firmly with the spatula once again. Cook for 1 minute, or until the cheese has melted completely. Remove from the pan and let cool for 5 minutes. Cut in half and serve.

For sandwich maker method: Preheat the sandwich maker. Follow directions for assembly above. Cook according to manufacturer's instructions.

Makes 4 sandwiches

Chapter 5

global grilled cheese

Welsh Rarebit

Even though we usually think of a grilled cheese sandwich as having two pieces of bread, this version is served open-face. You have the option of spooning the cheesy sauce over buttered toast and serving it just like that, or you can take it one step further and put the cheese toast under the broiler for a minute or two to create a brown and bubbly crust.

The two main types of rarebits (also known as rabbit) are one with a plain cheese sauce and one that has Worcestershire sauce and beer added. I have opted for the beer version here, which I happen to believe is the authentic one.

- 4 slices *pain au levain*, toasted (or use sourdough or Italian bread)
- 4 tablespoons butter
- 2 tablespoons all-purpose flour
- ½ cup bottled stout (such as Guinness)
- 1 tablespoon Worcestershire sauce
- 1 teaspoon dry mustard
- Pinch of cayenne pepper
- 8 ounces cheddar cheese, coarsely grated (preferably orange for the full effect; or use Gloucester or Cheshire)
- 8 slices cooked bacon (optional)
- 8 slices tomato, lightly salted (optional)

Place an oven rack about 6 inches below the heating element and preheat the broiler. Toast the bread on one side until golden brown. Turn the bread and butter with 2 tablespoons of the butter. Place in the broiler and toast until browned. Remove from the broiler and let cool.

To make the rarebit: In a medium saucepan, melt the remaining 2 tablespoons of butter over medium heat. Sprinkle the flour over the butter and whisk for 1 minute. Slowly whisk in the beer. When the foam subsides, whisk in the Worcestershire, mustard, and cayenne. Remove the pan from the heat, add the cheese, and stir until the sauce is smooth and creamy.

Place the bread on individual plates, buttered side up, and spoon enough of the cheese mixture over each slice to cover (you might have a little extra). Place the bacon and/or tomato slices on top of the cheese, and serve right away.

Alternatively, you can broil the sandwiches. To do so, place the bread in an ovenproof pan or on a baking sheet. Place the tomatoes and bacon on the bread and spoon a little cheese sauce on top. Broil the open-face sandwiches for 4 to 5 minutes, until brown and bubbly. Serve right away.

Makes 4 sandwiches

The Spaniard

Pimentón de la Vera is an ingredient that adds a haunting flavor to almost any dish. The Spanish smoky paprika can be found in sweet form (*dulce*), bittersweet and medium-hot (*agridulce*), or spicy (*picante*). You may use any of them for this sandwich.

- -

> 2 tablespoons butter, at room temperature
>
> ½ teaspoon *pimentón de la Vera*
>
> 8 slices sandwich-size Italian bread
>
> 8 thin slices serrano ham (about 3 ounces; or use prosciutto)
>
> 4 ounces young Mahón cheese, coarsely grated (or use fontina or American Muenster)
>
> 4 ounces manchego cheese, coarsely grated
>
> 4 piquillo peppers, stems removed, slit lengthwise, and opened like a book

In a small bowl, mix the butter and *pimentón* together.

To assemble: Spread the *pimentón*-butter mixture on one side of each of the bread slices. Place 4 slices of bread, buttered side down, on your work surface. Place 2 slices of ham on the bread. Distribute the cheeses over the ham. Lay the peppers over the cheese and top with the remaining bread slices, buttered side up.

For stovetop method: Heat a large nonstick skillet over medium heat for 2 minutes. Put the sandwiches into the pan, cover, and cook for 3 to 4 minutes, until the undersides are golden brown. Remove the cover and turn the sandwiches, pressing each one firmly with a spatula to compress the filling slightly. Cover and cook for 2 to 3 minutes, until the undersides are well browned. Turn the sandwiches once more, press firmly with the spatula again, cook for 1 minute, and remove from the pan. Let cool for 2 to 3 minutes. Cut in half and serve.

For sandwich maker method: Preheat the sandwich maker. Follow directions for assembly above. Cook according to manufacturer's instructions.

Makes 4 sandwiches

Arepas with Monterey Jack, Plantains, and Black Beans

The filled corn flour dough "sandwiches" known as arepas are found in many Central and South American countries, although each country has its own version. While making arepas takes a little more time than making a typical grilled cheese sandwich, once you learn to make them you'll learn how easy they really are. You can find arepa flour, usually marketed as precooked (or *precocida*) corn flour, in most Latin American markets. If all else fails, use English muffins.

. . . .

Arepas
> 1 cup arepa flour (called masarepa, precooked corn flour, or
>   precocida; do *not* use instant masa or masa harina)
>
> 4 ounces Monterey Jack cheese, coarsely grated
>
> ¼ cup fresh or frozen corn, blanched in boiling water for 3 minutes
>   and drained
>
> 1 teaspoon sugar
>
> ½ teaspoon salt
>
> 1 cup lukewarm water
>
> 2 teaspoons vegetable oil

Plantains

    1 tablespoon butter

    2 teaspoons vegetable oil

    1 ripe plantain (a ripe plantain will be almost black), sliced on the diagonal ¼ inch thick

    Salt

Beans

    2 teaspoons vegetable oil

    ¼ cup finely chopped onion (about 2 ounces)

    ½ cup canned black beans, drained

    ¼ teaspoon ground cumin

    ½ teaspoon salt

    ½ teaspoon freshly ground black pepper

    8 ounces Monterey Jack cheese, coarsely grated

To make the arepas: Mix together the flour, cheese, corn, sugar, and salt in a medium bowl. Slowly add the water and stir until the mixture is moist and holds together. Cover and let sit for 15 minutes. This will allow the flour to absorb the liquid. If it seems dry, add water a few drops at a time.

Divide the dough into 4 pieces. Roll each piece into a ball and then flatten into a disk measuring approximately 3 inches in diameter and ¾ inch thick.

To cook the arepas, heat the oil in a large nonstick skillet over medium heat. Line a plate with paper towels. Add the arepas to the skillet and cook without disturbing for 5 to 6 minutes, or until the cakes are deep golden brown and splotchy on the bottom. Turn and cook the other sides, also until deep golden brown and splotchy. Transfer to the plate to drain. Wipe out the skillet with a paper towel but do not wash it.

To make the plantains: Heat the butter and oil in a medium nonstick skillet over medium-high heat. Line a plate with paper towels. Add the plantain slices to the skillet and cook until caramelized and golden brown around the edges, 2 to 3 minutes on each side. Salt very lightly and transfer to the plate to cool. Wipe out the skillet with a paper towel but do not wash it.

To make the beans: Heat the vegetable oil in the same skillet you used to make the plantains. Add the onion and cook until soft, about 5 minutes. Add the beans, cumin, salt, and pepper and cook until the beans are heated through, about 5 minutes. Transfer to a bowl and use the back of a fork to mash the beans. This will help the beans stay on the arepas instead of falling out when you flip them.

To assemble: Use a serrated knife and carefully cut each arepa in half horizontally. Place 4 arepa halves, cut side up, on your work surface. Place about 2 tablespoons of the black bean mixture on the arepas. Follow with a few plantain slices. Distribute the cheese over the top. You may have to use your palms to compress the cheese to make it fit. (Don't worry if some of the cheese strands fall by the wayside.) Top with the remaining arepa halves, cut side down.

For stovetop method: Heat the same skillet you used to make the arepas over medium-low heat for 2 minutes. Place the filled arepas in the pan, cover, and cook for about 5 minutes, or until the cheese has begun to melt and the bottoms are a deep golden brown. Carefully turn, cover, and cook for 4 to 5 minutes, until the cheese has completely melted. (You might need to peek inside to make sure.) Remove from the heat and let cool for 5 minutes. Cut in half or serve whole. (Depending on your arepas, these can be a little messy. As a result, you might want to serve them with a knife and fork just to be sure.)

For sandwich maker method: These cannot be made in a sandwich maker because the arepas are too delicate to withstand the weight of the top of the griddle.

NOTE: One of the great things about arepas is how versatile they are. You can fill them with pulled pork, chicken or grilled flank steak, a little cheese, and a drizzle of Mexican crema or crème fraîche. Or you can forget the meat and fill them with one or two cheeses, a little cilantro and onion, and a sprinkling of chopped black olives. No matter what, you're in for one great sandwich, Latin American style.

Makes 4 sandwiches

Cubano

Some say that a Cubano isn't a Cubano unless it's made in either Miami or Tampa, Florida (or Cuba, of course). But you can't keep a good sandwich down, and because of that, you can find Cuban sandwiches all over America. Making an authentic one, however, means thinking ahead. You have to marinate the pork for 24 hours and then cook it the next day for about 2 hours. Also, authentic Cuban rolls are hard to find outside of Florida, so use sub rolls or sandwich rolls instead.

Finally, a Cubano isn't a Cubano if it isn't pressed. That means this is the time to break out your sandwich maker if you have one. Otherwise, see instructions below for how to replicate the effects of a sandwich maker on your stovetop.

- -

8 ounces Swiss cheese, coarsely grated

8 cornichons, coarsely chopped

4 crusty sandwich rolls or sub rolls

4 tablespoons butter, at room temperature

4 (2-ounce) slices Cuban Pork (recipe follows)

4 (1-ounce) slices ham (such as Black Forest)

Yellow mustard (optional)

In a small bowl, mix together the cheese and cornichons.

Split the sandwich rolls in half and butter the crust sides as well as the insides. Place the flat (bottom) half, cut side up, on your work surface. Layer the pork, ham, and cheese mixture on the bread. Spread the mustard on the cut side of the top half of the rolls. Turn the tops, cut side down, and place on top of the filling.

Heat a large nonstick skillet over medium-low heat. Place the sandwiches in the pan. Instead of covering, put a heavy skillet, such as cast iron, or a skillet with a heavy can, such as canned tomatoes, on top of the sandwiches to compress them. This is key to a Cubano. Cook for 3 to 4 minutes, until the undersides are well browned. Turn the sandwiches and place the cast-iron pan on top to further compress the sandwiches. Cook for about 3 minutes, or until the bread is well browned. Turn once more, compress with a spatula, and cook for 1 more minute, or until the cheese has completely melted. Let cool for 5 minutes. Cut in half and serve.

For sandwich maker method: The Cubano is tailor-made for the sandwich maker. Preheat the sandwich maker. Follow directions for assembly above. Cook according to manufacturer's instructions.

Makes 4 sandwiches

· ·

Cuban Pork

 1¼ cups freshly squeezed orange juice

 ¼ cup freshly squeezed lemon juice

 ¼ cup freshly squeezed lime juice

 ¼ cup olive oil

 10 cloves garlic, minced

 1 tablespoon kosher salt

 1 tablespoon finely chopped fresh oregano

 ½ teaspoon freshly ground black pepper

 1 (4- to 5-pound) boneless pork shoulder (also called pork butt), surface fat trimmed

Whisk together the orange, lemon, and lime juices and olive oil in a medium bowl.

Put the garlic, salt, oregano, and pepper in a small bowl. Use the back of a fork or a pestle to make a paste.

Use the tip of a knife to make ¼-inch slits all over the meat. Rub the meat with the garlic paste. Put the meat in a large plastic bag. Pour the juice mixture into the bag and gently rock the bag to make sure the juice mixture coats the meat. Place the meat in a larger plastic bag or in a large roasting pan to prevent unwanted spills. Refrigerate for 24 hours, turning the meat occasionally to make sure the meat is thoroughly marinated.

When ready to cook, take the meat out of the refrigerator about 45 minutes before cooking to allow it to come to room temperature. Preheat the oven to 325°F.

Take the meat out of the bag and place in a roasting pan just large enough to hold it. Discard the marinade. Roast for about 2 hours, or until an instant-read thermometer reaches 155°F when inserted in the thickest part of the meat. Let rest until cool enough to cut slices for sandwiches. Or, if serving hot, loosely cover the meat with aluminum foil and let rest for about 20 minutes before slicing.

Makes enough for about 24 sandwiches or 6 to 8 entrée servings

The Greek

This sandwich is a riff on the Greek spinach and cheese–filled pastry called spanakopita. But instead of the phyllo dough typically used to encase the filling, this recipe naturally calls for bread. In that way, this is probably not something you'll find in Greece, but the combination of tangy feta and spinach will almost certainly still make you think of that special Mediterranean country.

1 tablespoon olive oil

1 large leek, white and light green parts only, sliced ¼ inch thick (or use 1 small yellow onion)

2 small cloves garlic, minced

4 ounces baby spinach (about 4 cups lightly packed; or use arugula)

2 ounces feta cheese, crumbled

Salt and freshly ground black pepper

2 tablespoons butter, at room temperature

8 sandwich-size slices French bread (or use sourdough or Italian)

8 ounces Gouda cheese, coarsely grated (or use Havarti, Monterey Jack, or Swiss)

Heat the oil in a large nonstick skillet over medium heat. Add the leek and cook until soft and just beginning to brown, 6 to 8 minutes. Add the garlic and cook for 1 minute, stirring continuously to make sure it doesn't burn. Add the spinach and cook until wilted but still bright green, about 3 minutes. Transfer the mixture to a medium bowl and let cool slightly. Add the feta and mix well. Salt very lightly to taste (the feta is salty, so you won't need much) and add a few grinds of pepper to taste. Wipe out the skillet with a paper towel but do not wash it.

To assemble: Butter one side of each slice of bread. Place 4 slices, buttered side down, on your work surface. Distribute the spinach mixture over them and follow with the Gouda. Top with the remaining bread slices, buttered side up.

For stovetop method: Heat a large nonstick skillet over medium heat for 2 minutes. Put the sandwiches into the pan, cover, and cook for 2 to 3 minutes, until the undersides are golden brown. Turn the sandwiches, pressing each one firmly with a spatula to flatten slightly. Cover and cook for 2 to 3 minutes, until the undersides are well browned. Remove the cover, turn the sandwiches once more, and press firmly with the spatula once again. Cook for 1 minute, or until the cheese has melted completely. (You may need to peek inside one of the sandwiches to make sure.) Remove from the pan and let cool for 5 minutes. Cut in half and serve.

For sandwich maker method: Preheat the sandwich maker. Follow directions for assembly above. Cook according to manufacturer's instructions.

Makes 4 sandwiches

Monte Cristo Sandwich

This sandwich combines the world's two best comfort foods—grilled cheese sandwiches and French toast—all in one bite.

The method for making this sandwich parts ways with the others in this book for two reasons: First, you slice rather than grate the cheese. That's because dipping the sandwiches in the egg mixture is a messy affair, and if the cheese is grated, you'll end up with more cheese in the egg mixture than on your sandwich. Second, there's no reason to butter the bread. You will, however, add butter to the pan so that the egg-coated bread won't stick and also so that the sandwiches have plenty of flavor.

- -

3 large eggs

⅓ cup milk

¼ teaspoon salt

8 sandwich-size slices brioche, egg bread, challah, or white bread

2 tablespoons yellow mustard

4 (1-ounce) slices cooked turkey

8 ounces Emmentaler or Swiss cheese, cut into 16 thin slices

4 (1-ounce) slices ham

2 tablespoons butter

Confectioners' sugar, for dusting

¼ cup strawberry jam (or use cherry, apricot, or any other jam you like)

In a shallow bowl large enough for the sandwiches to fit, whisk together the eggs, milk, and salt.

To assemble: Place all 8 bread slices on your work surface. Spread the mustard on each piece of bread. Layer the turkey on 4 slices of bread, followed by the cheese and then the ham. Top with the remaining bread slices.

For stovetop method: Heat the butter in a large nonstick skillet over medium heat. Dip each sandwich into the egg mixture, turning to coat both sides. Transfer the sandwiches to the pan. Cover and cook for 3 to 4 minutes, until the undersides begin to brown. Turn the sandwiches and press lightly with a spatula to compress the filling slightly. Cover and cook for about 3 minutes, or until the bread is golden brown. (Watch carefully, because the delicate bread can burn easily.) Turn once more and cook for 1 to 2 minutes, until the cheese has melted completely. Let stand for 5 minutes. Sprinkle with confectioners' sugar. Cut diagonally in half and serve with a dollop of jam alongside.

For sandwich maker method: This sandwich does not lend itself to being prepared in a sandwich maker.

Makes 4 sandwiches

Chapter 6

grilled cheese
on the go

Jalapeño Popper

The American Grilled Cheese Kitchen

The American Grilled Cheese Kitchen in San Francisco is a phenomenon in almost every respect. Co-owner Heidi Gibson won seven consecutive titles at the annual Grilled Cheese Invitational, an unprecedented feat; there had never been a stand-alone grilled cheese restaurant in San Francisco, and neither she nor co-owner Nate Pollak had restaurant experience. But Heidi and Nate took all those contest wins as a sign that maybe they should turn a passion into a business. And so they did. Ever since opening their doors in June 2010, people have been lining up to taste sandwiches like this fiery Jalapeño Popper, as well as every other creative and delicious sandwich they've invented. For grilled cheese lovers, a trip to San Francisco would not be complete without a visit to The American.

- -

8 slices bacon

2 tablespoons butter, at room temperature

8 slices *pain au levain* (or use Italian or sourdough bread)

3 ounces fresh goat cheese, at room temperature

8 tablespoons Jalapeño Relish (recipe follows)

8 ounces Monterey Jack cheese, coarsely grated

Line a plate with paper towels. Place the bacon in a large nonstick skillet and cook over medium heat until browned and crisp. Transfer to the plate to cool. Break each piece in half. Drain the fat from the pan. Wipe out the skillet with a paper towel but do not wash it.

To assemble: Spread butter on each slice of bread. Place all 8 slices, buttered side down, on your work surface. Spread the goat cheese on 4 of the slices and the relish on the others. Distribute the Monterey Jack on the side with the relish, followed by the bacon strips. Top with the remaining bread slices, goat cheese side down.

For stovetop method: Heat a large nonstick skillet over medium heat for 2 minutes. Put the sandwiches into the pan, cover, and cook for 3 to 4 minutes, until the undersides are golden brown. Turn the sandwiches, pressing each one firmly with a spatula to flatten slightly. Cover and cook for 3 to 4 minutes, until the undersides are well browned. Remove the cover, turn the sandwiches once more, and press firmly with the spatula once again. Cook for 1 minute, or until the cheese has melted completely. Remove from the pan and let cool for 5 minutes. Cut in half and serve.

For sandwich maker method: Preheat the sandwich maker. Follow directions for assembly above. Cook according to manufacturer's instructions.

Makes 4 sandwiches

Jalapeño Relish

4 ounces dried California apricots (if possible, do not use Turkish), coarsely chopped

¾ cup finely chopped white onion (3 ounces)

1 large or 2 small fresh jalapeño chiles, stems removed, seeded, and minced

1 fresh serrano chile, stems removed, seeded, and minced

¼ teaspoon fresh habanero chile (add only if you want to make your relish incendiary)

1 tablespoon minced fresh ginger

1½ teaspoons freshly squeezed lime juice

¾ teaspoon dry mustard

1½ teaspoons apple cider vinegar

½ teaspoon salt

Mix all of the ingredients together thoroughly in a medium bowl and allow to sit for at least 1 hour but preferably overnight, refrigerated.

NATE'S NOTE: The amount of chiles may be adjusted to taste so that nobody burns their face off, but we've found that the cheese and bacon really knock the heat down. In other words, make the relish hotter than you think you'd want it.

Makes about ¼ cup

Brie's Company

Hammontree's

Chad Hammontree had been cooking for a long time when he decided he wanted to open a soup place. He created a few grilled cheese sandwiches to go with the soups, but he quickly realized that grilled cheese should be the focus instead of soup. So in 2009 he and his wife, Alison, opened the doors to Hammontree's in Fayetteville, Arkansas. You'll still find plenty of soups on the menu, but grilled cheese is the star. So too are clever creations and the names that go with them, as evidenced by this recipe title.

With this recipe, Chad's idea was to re-create the popular hors d'oeuvre Brie *en croûte*. Note that although he provides the method for making fig jam, if you're able to find fig jam in your market, go ahead and use it. Just make sure it has no added spices.

Fig Jam

    8 dried figs (about 2½ ounces), stems removed

    6 ounces apple or currant jelly

Caramelized Onions

    1 tablespoon butter

    1 large onion, thinly sliced lengthwise

    6 ounces light-bodied beer (such as lager)

    Salt and freshly ground black pepper

    4 ounces Gouda cheese, coarsely grated

    4 ounces Monterey Jack cheese, coarsely grated

    3 ounces Asiago cheese, coarsely grated

    2 tablespoons butter, at room temperature

    8 slices sourdough bread (Chad's note: Use real sourdough, not the
        soft white lunch bread sometimes called sourdough.)

    1 large or 2 small Granny Smith apples, cored and cut into 16
        (¼-inch-thick) slices

    8 ounces double-cream Brie cheese, sliced ¼ inch thick

To make the fig jam: Put figs and jelly in the bowl of a food processor. Process until smooth. Set aside. (Can be made 1 week in advance and refrigerated.)

To make the onions: Place 1 tablespoon butter in a large nonstick skillet over medium-high heat. Add the onions and cook, stirring occasionally, until deep golden brown, 8 to 10 minutes. Add the beer, and stir constantly until the liquid cooks away. (Chad's note: Drink the other half of the beer.) Add salt and pepper to taste. Transfer to a plate. Wipe out the skillet with a paper towel, but do not wash it.

While the onions are cooking, make the apples.

In a medium bowl, mix together the Gouda, Monterey Jack, and Asiago cheeses.

To assemble: Butter one side of each slice of bread. Place 4 slices, buttered side down, on your work surface. Spread each slice with 1½ tablespoons fig jam (you may have a little left over). Lay the apple slices on the jam. Follow with the mixed cheeses. You'll need to press fairly firmly with your hand to compress all that cheese. Place the onions on top of the cheese and follow with the Brie slices. Top with the remaining bread, buttered side up.

For stovetop method: Heat the same skillet you used to make the onions over medium heat for 2 minutes. Put the sandwiches into the pan, cover, and cook for 3 to 4 minutes, until the undersides are golden brown. Turn the sandwiches, pressing each one firmly with a spatula to flatten slightly. Cover and cook for 3 to 4 minutes, until the undersides are well browned. Remove the cover, turn the sandwiches once more, and press firmly with the spatula once again. Cook for 1 minute, or until the cheese has melted completely. Remove from the pan and let cool for 5 minutes. Cut in half and serve.

For sandwich maker method: Preheat the sandwich maker. Follow directions for assembly above. Cook according to manufacturer's instructions.

Makes 4 sandwiches

The Sweetest Thing

Grilled Cheese & Company

The founders of Grilled Cheese & Company, in Catonsville, Maryland, got their start by firing up grilled cheese sandwiches at beer and wine festivals, some of which were attended by as many as 30,000 people. The long lines every time convinced them they needed to open a permanent place. And so they did.

This recipe is the only sweet one on their menu, and when you taste it you'll understand why it stands alone. Very few combinations are better than the marriage of creamy Brie, raspberries, rich mascarpone, and chocolate.

- -

6 ounces mascarpone cheese

2 tablespoons raspberry preserves

2 tablespoons butter, at room temperature

8 sandwich-size slices egg bread, challah, or brioche

8 ounces Brie cheese, sliced ¼ inch thick

¼ cup regular or mini semisweet chocolate chips

In a small bowl, combine the mascarpone and preserves and mix well.

To assemble: Butter one side of each slice of bread. Place 4 slices of bread, buttered side down, on your work surface. Spread the mascarpone mixture on the bread. Lay the Brie slices over the mixture and sprinkle with the chocolate chips. Top with the remaining slices of bread, buttered side up.

For stovetop method: Heat a large nonstick skillet over medium heat for 2 minutes. Put the sandwiches into the pan, cover, and cook for 2 to 3 minutes, until the undersides are golden brown. (Watch carefully, because egg bread burns easily.) Turn the sandwiches, pressing each one firmly with a spatula to flatten slightly. Cover and cook for 2 to 3 minutes, until the undersides are well browned. Remove the cover, turn the sandwiches once more, and press firmly with the spatula once again. Cook for 1 minute, or until the cheese has melted completely. Remove from the pan and let cool for 2 to 3 minutes. Cut in half and serve.

For sandwich maker method: If your sandwich maker lid is quite heavy and you cannot adjust its weight, you should not use the sandwich maker for this sandwich. The filling is too creamy and will end up oozing out. Otherwise, preheat the sandwich maker. Follow directions for assembly above. Cook according to manufacturer's instructions.

Makes 4 sandwiches

Harvest Melt

The Grilled Cheese Truck

Combining a love of food and extensive cooking experience, The Grilled Cheese Truck owners, Dave Danhi and Michele Grant, entered the 2009 Grilled Cheese Invitational in Los Angeles on a whim. Their sandwich, the Cheesy Mac 'n' Rib, didn't win, but the sight of a truck parked nearby served as inspiration to mount their passion on four wheels and set up a roadside shop. The Grilled Cheese Truck in Los Angeles has been a huge hit ever since.

Their signature Cheesy Mac 'n' Rib is their most popular sandwich, but the simpler and, I daresay, healthier Harvest Melt is equally popular because of its seductive combination of roasted butternut squash, leeks, cheese, and a couple of surprising sweet elements.

Squash
> 1 small butternut squash (preferably with a long thin neck)
> Olive oil, for brushing

Leeks

1½ tablespoons butter

2 medium leeks, white and light green parts only, sliced ¼ inch thick

1 teaspoon finely chopped fresh thyme

Salt and freshly ground black pepper

2 teaspoons balsamic syrup (see Note)

2 tablespoons butter, at room temperature

8 slices whole-grain bread

8 ounces Gruyère cheese, coarsely grated (or use Comté or Swiss)

1 tablespoon agave nectar

To make the squash: Preheat the oven to 425°F.

Peel and cut the neck portion of the squash into 8 (¼-inch-thick) slices. (If the neck isn't long enough to yield the 8 slices you need, simply cut ¼-inch-thick slices from the wider portion of the squash and cut them in half crosswise.)

Place the squash slices on a baking sheet and brush with oil. Roast for 15 to 20 minutes, turning halfway through, until the slices are starting to brown on the edges. Let cool.

To make the leeks: Heat the butter in a large nonstick skillet over medium-high heat. Add the leeks and cook until soft and just beginning to brown around the edges, 8 to 10 minutes. Stir in the thyme and salt and pepper to taste. Transfer the leeks to a plate. Wipe out the skillet with a paper towel but do not wash it.

To assemble: Brush both sides of the squash with the balsamic syrup. Butter one side of each slice of bread. Place 4 slices of bread, buttered side down, on your work surface. Put 2 slices of squash on each piece of bread. Follow with half of the cheese and the leeks. Distribute the remaining cheese on top of the leeks. Drizzle with the agave nectar. Top with the remaining bread slices, buttered side up.

For stovetop method: Heat a large nonstick skillet over medium heat for 2 minutes. Put the sandwiches into the pan, cover, and cook for 3 to 4 minutes, until the undersides are golden brown. Turn the sandwiches, pressing each one firmly with a spatula to flatten slightly. Cover and cook for 3 to 4 minutes, until the undersides are well browned. Remove the cover, turn the sandwiches once more, and press firmly with the spatula once again. Cook for 1 minute, or until the cheese has melted completely. Remove from the pan and let cool for 5 minutes. Cut in half and serve.

For sandwich maker method: Preheat the sandwich maker. Follow directions for assembly above. Cook according to manufacturer's instructions.

NOTE: Balsamic syrup is easily found in the supermarket, on or near the same shelves as the balsamic vinegar.

Makes 4 sandwiches

Milk Truck Market Sandwich

The Milk Truck

If you catch up with Keith Klein and the Milk Truck at the Brooklyn Flea in Brooklyn, New York, you'll be handsomely rewarded with crisp panini encasing great cheeses along with ingredients like homemade olive spread, arugula pesto, or the feta salsa verde that follows in this excellent recipe.

Here is Keith's note about the feta salsa verde: "The basic recipe calls for some sort of herb (in this case, parsley), shallots, something pickled, some kind of acid (lemon, vinegar), and olive oil. You can vary this depending on what herbs, pickled things, and acid you have on hand. You can add Dijon mustard if you want it thicker, or cooked egg yolk. One note: Be sure the parsley is completely dry before you chop it to ensure the brightest flavor." Keith also uses shallot oil to brush the outside of the bread, but I've simplified the recipe a tad by using olive oil instead.

Feta Salsa Verde

½ cup packed fresh Italian parsley leaves, finely chopped

½ large shallot, finely chopped (about 2 tablespoons)

½ cup finely chopped scallions (or use ½ large leek, white and light green parts only)

1 tablespoon capers, rinsed, drained, and chopped

1 anchovy fillet, minced (optional)

¼ teaspoon red pepper flakes

¼ cup olive oil

2 teaspoons finely grated lemon zest

2 tablespoons freshly squeezed lemon juice

1½ teaspoons red wine vinegar

2 ounces feta cheese, crumbled

Salt and freshly ground black pepper

Sandwiches

4 tablespoons olive oil

4 sandwich rolls

8 ounces fresh mozzarella cheese, sliced ¼ inch thick

8 (¼-inch-thick) slices heirloom or beefsteak tomato

Salt and freshly ground black pepper

To make the salsa: Put the parsley, shallot, scallions, capers, anchovy, and red pepper flakes in a medium bowl. Stir in the oil, lemon zest, lemon juice, and vinegar. Add the feta and mix well. Add salt and pepper to taste, bearing in mind that the feta is salty. If the mixture seems dry, add a little more olive oil. You want it to be runny enough to spread but thick enough to stay on the sandwich.

To assemble: Split the sandwich rolls in half lengthwise if they aren't already. Place them, crust side up, on your work surface and brush with the shallot oil. Turn the flat (bottom) halves of the rolls, cut side up. Spread about 2 tablespoons of the feta salsa on each half. Follow with the mozzarella. Lay the tomatoes on top of the cheese and sprinkle with a little salt and pepper. Top with the remaining roll halves, crust side up.

For stovetop method: Heat a large nonstick skillet over medium-low heat for 2 minutes. Put the sandwiches into the pan, cover, and cook for 3 to 4 minutes, until the undersides are golden brown. Turn the sandwiches, pressing each one firmly with a spatula to compress the filling. Cover and cook for 3 to 4 minutes, until the undersides are well browned and the cheese has begun to melt. Remove the cover, turn the sandwiches once more, and press firmly with the spatula once again. Cook for 1 to 2 minutes, until the cheese has melted completely. (You might need to peek inside to make sure.) Remove from the pan and let cool for 2 to 3 minutes. Cut in half and serve.

For sandwich maker method: Preheat the sandwich maker. Follow directions for assembly above. Cook according to manufacturer's instructions.

Makes 4 sandwiches

The Cheesus Burger

THE GRiLLeD CHeeSe GRiLL™ PDX

Grilled Cheese Grill

This grilled cheese–hamburger combination comes to us by way of Portland, Oregon's Grilled Cheese Grill and its owner, Matt Breslow. A snowy Christmas and a few snowed-in hungry cousins inspired Matt's creation, which is now the main attraction at his popular eatery. Almost as good as the sandwiches is the place he has set up as his dining area—a non-operational school bus outfitted with tables, condiments, and plenty of napkins.

This explanation of the Cheesus Burger comes directly from Matt: "For this behemoth of a cheeseburger, the traditional burger bun is replaced by two grilled cheese sandwiches holding the burger and fixin's between them, with a twist. For recommended bread choice, think Wonder Bread. Use something airy and smaller than your normal deli-style wide loaf, since you will want the bread to crush down a bit and not dominate the taste of the burger."

Oh, and the name? Well, it was Christmas, after all.

1⅓ pounds ground beef

1½ teaspoons kosher salt

½ teaspoon freshly ground black pepper

2 teaspoons vegetable oil

1 small sweet onion (such as Walla Walla or Vidalia), thinly sliced

2 tablespoons butter, at room temperature

16 slices white or wheat bread

8 slices American cheese

4 dill pickles, cut into 5 lengthwise strips each (or use sandwich stackers)

8 slices Colby-Jack cheese, about 6 ounces

1 tablespoon plus 1 teaspoon ketchup

1 tablespoon plus 1 teaspoon ballpark-style mustard

8 iceberg lettuce leaves

1 large tomato, cut into 8 (¼-inch-thick) slices

Preheat the oven to 300°F.

In a medium bowl, mix the beef with the salt and pepper. Form into 4 fairly thin patties about ½ inch thick. Set aside.

Heat the oil in a large nonstick skillet over medium-high heat. Add the onions and cook until soft but not brown, about 5 minutes. Transfer to a plate. Wipe out the skillet with a paper towel but do not wash it.

To assemble the sandwiches: Butter one side of each slice of bread. Place the bread on your work surface, buttered side down. Put 1 American cheese slice on 4 pieces of bread and follow with the pickles. Place another American cheese slice on top of the pickles. Top with 4 slices of bread, buttered side up.

Put 1 slice of Colby-Jack on 4 other pieces of bread. Distribute the onions and top with another slice of Colby-Jack. Top with the remaining bread slices, buttered side up.

To cook the sandwiches: Heat the same skillet you used for the onions over medium heat for 2 minutes. Place the sandwiches in the pan, in batches if necessary, cover, and cook for 3 to 4 minutes, until the undersides are golden brown. Turn the sandwiches and press lightly with a spatula to compress the filling. Cover and cook for 2 to 3 minutes, until the undersides are well browned. Remove the cover, turn once more, and cook until the cheese has completely melted. Transfer the sandwiches to a baking sheet and place in the oven.

To make the hamburgers: Heat a large skillet or griddle over medium-high heat for 2 minutes. Put the hamburgers in the pan and cook for about 6 minutes, or until the edges of the patties begin to brown and the juices start to run. Turn the patties and cook for 4 to 5 minutes for medium-rare and 6 to 7 minutes for medium-well.

To assemble: Place the sandwiches on a large cutting board or other work surface. You will now use them as you would two sides of a burger bun. Spread the ketchup on top of the American cheese sandwiches and the mustard on top of the Colby-Jack ones. Place the burger on the American cheese side, followed by the lettuce and tomato. Top with the Colby-Jack sandwich. Follow Matt's note on page 116 and serve.

MATT'S NOTE: "Cut it corner to corner and marvel at the cross section momentarily before plating it, ideally with a bag of chips and an ice-cold pickle spear."

For sandwich maker method: Although you can use a sandwich maker to make these, the number of steps involved may make it too complicated.

Makes 4 sandwiches

Chapter 7

regional american grilled cheese

Pimento Grilled Cheese

A trip to the magnificent Blackberry Farm in Walland, Tennessee, convinced me that as a Californian, I'd grown up without one of the most important yet basic cheese-related foods ever invented: pimento cheese. The Blackberry Farm version uses their flagship sheep's milk cheese called Singing Brook, but the recipe is no less spectacular with cheddar. The celery is my nod to the oft-found accompaniment to pimento cheese.

¾ cup Pimento Cheese from Blackberry Farm (recipe follows)
½ cup coarsely chopped celery
2 tablespoons butter, at room temperature
8 slices brioche (or use egg bread or challah)

In a medium bowl, mix together the pimento cheese and celery.

To assemble: Spread butter on one side of each slice of bread. Place 4 slices of bread, buttered side down, on your work surface. Spread the cheese mixture on the bread. Top with the remaining bread slices, buttered side up.

For stovetop method: Heat a large nonstick skillet over medium-low heat for 2 minutes. Put the sandwiches into the pan, cover, and cook for 3 to 4 minutes, until the undersides are golden brown. Turn the sandwiches, pressing each one firmly with a spatula to flatten slightly. Cover and cook for 2 to 3 minutes, until the undersides are well browned. Remove the cover, turn the sandwiches once more, and press firmly with the spatula once again. Cook for 1 minute, or until the cheese is warmed through completely and the bread is crisp. Remove from the pan and let cool for 5 minutes. Cut in half and serve.

For sandwich maker method: Preheat the sandwich maker. Follow directions for assembly above. Cook according to manufacturer's instructions.

Makes 4 sandwiches

▪ ▪

Pimento Cheese from Blackberry Farm

1 teaspoon finely chopped garlic

6 tablespoons mayonnaise

2 tablespoons dill pickle brine

1½ teaspoons Dijon mustard

1 teaspoon Frank's RedHot sauce (or use your favorite hot sauce)

½ teaspoon salt

¼ teaspoon freshly ground black pepper

⅓ cup finely chopped red bell peppers (or use red pimentos from a jar, drained)

1 pound cheddar cheese (preferably aged), finely grated

In a medium bowl, mix together the garlic, mayonnaise, pickle brine, mustard, hot sauce, salt, and black pepper. Stir in the red peppers and cheese, and mix well.

NOTE: This recipe makes more than you will need for the sandwiches. Serve the extra with celery sticks or crackers. It will keep, refrigerated, for about 2 weeks.

Makes about 3 cups

Philly Cheese Steak

Because of the thick bread used to make a cheese steak, this is the time to break out your sandwich maker if you have one; or use weights as described on page xiv.

- -

12 ounces skirt steak

¾ teaspoon salt

½ teaspoon freshly ground black pepper

½ teaspoon garlic powder

¼ cup olive oil

1 medium onion, sliced ¼ inch thick

1 medium red bell pepper, seeded and sliced ¼ inch thick

8 ounces white or brown mushrooms, stems removed and sliced ¼ inch thick

2 cloves garlic, minced

4 mini baguettes, sub rolls, or crusty Italian rolls, split in half horizontally

8 ounces medium-sharp provolone cheese, coarsely grated

Place the meat in the freezer for 10 minutes. (This will make it easier to slice.) Cut the meat against the grain into very thin slices, about ⅛ inch thick.

In a medium bowl, mix together the meat, salt, pepper, and garlic powder. Set aside.

Heat 2 tablespoons of the oil in a large nonstick skillet over medium heat. Add the onion and bell pepper and cook just until soft, about 5 minutes. Add the mushrooms and cook for 2 minutes. Add the garlic and cook until the mushrooms are soft and just beginning to darken around the edges, about 3 minutes. Transfer the mixture to a plate. Wipe out the skillet with a paper towel but do not wash it.

Heat a medium skillet over medium heat and add the meat. Cook, stirring constantly, until the meat is cooked through and no longer showing pink, about 5 minutes. (If you like your meat on the rare side, however, then you can deviate from the Philly style and cook the meat for a shorter period of time.)

To assemble: Pinch the soft centers out of each piece of bread to create a well. Place the bread, crust side up, on your work surface and brush with the remaining 2 tablespoons oil. Turn 4 pieces of bread, oil side down, on your work surface and distribute the meat over them. Follow with the onion-pepper mixture and then the cheese. Top with the remaining bread slices, oil side up.

For stovetop method: Heat the same nonstick skillet you used to make the onion mixture over medium-low to medium heat for 2 minutes. (If your stove runs hot, turn the heat even lower.) Put the sandwiches in the pan, cover, and cook for 6 to 7 minutes, or until the bread is evenly browned. Turn the sandwiches, pressing each one firmly with a spatula to compress the bread and filling. Cover and cook for 5 to 6 minutes, until the undersides are well browned. Turn the sandwiches once more, press firmly with the spatula again, cover, and cook for 1 to 2 more minutes, until the cheese has thoroughly melted. Remove from the pan and let cool for 5 minutes. Cut in half and serve.

For sandwich maker method: Preheat the sandwich maker. Follow directions for assembly above. Cook according to manufacturer's instructions.

Makes 4 sandwiches

The Californian

California is known for its agricultural bounty, and this sandwich reflects that. The California raisin and almond crops are the biggest in the country. Goat cheese got on the national map because of California producer Laura Chenel, and Monterey Jack was invented in California. The chile reflects the vibrant and vital Mexican culture and also adds great flavor. Combined in a grilled cheese sandwich, these ingredients, including the iconic Humboldt Fog cheese, create a memorable sandwich and a true taste of the Golden State.

- -

4 ounces Humboldt Fog cheese, at room temperature (or use any bloomy-rind or fresh goat cheese)

1 canned chipotle chile en adobo, finely chopped

3 tablespoons butter, at room temperature

8 slices cinnamon-raisin bread

2 tablespoons plus 2 teaspoons sliced almonds

8 ounces Monterey Jack cheese

In a small bowl, mash the goat cheese and chile together.

To assemble: Spread butter on one side of each of the bread slices. Carefully but firmly press the almonds onto the butter. Place 4 slices of bread, buttered side down, on your work surface. Spread the goat cheese mixture on each slice of bread. Follow with the Monterey Jack. Use your hands to compress it if necessary. Top with the remaining bread slices, buttered side up.

For stovetop method: Heat a large nonstick skillet over medium heat for 2 minutes. Put the sandwiches into the pan, cover, and cook for 2 to 3 minutes, until golden brown. Turn the sandwiches, pressing each one firmly

with a spatula to flatten slightly. Cover and cook for 2 to 3 minutes, until the undersides are well browned. Turn the sandwiches once more, press firmly with the spatula again, cook for 1 minute, and remove from the pan. Let cool for 5 minutes. Cut in half and serve.

For sandwich maker method: Preheat the sandwich maker. Follow directions for assembly above. Cook according to manufacturer's instructions.

Makes 4 sandwiches

The Vermonter

Vermont is home to the largest number of sheep's milk cheese producers in the country. The sheep are able to withstand the harsh winters, and they enjoy the rich summer pastures. But goats do just fine in Vermont too, and that's why there are some amazing goat's milk cheeses coming out of the Green Mountain State. When it comes to cheese, though, Vermont is known most of all for its cheddar, as well it should be. It has a long cheddar history, and to this day some of the best cheddars in America are made there. In addition to cheese, Vermont is well known for its maple syrup, which is why it appears in this recipe.

2 ounces goat cheese, at room temperature

2 teaspoons maple syrup

2 tablespoons butter, at room temperature

8 sandwich-size slices walnut bread (or use country white or sourdough)

4 ounces Vermont cheddar cheese (such as Cabot Clothbound or Grafton Bandage-Wrapped), coarsely grated

4 ounces Vermont Shepherd cheese, coarsely grated (or use Petit Basque, Ossau-Iraty, or other mountain-style sheep's milk cheese)

In a small bowl, mix the goat cheese and maple syrup together.

To assemble: Spread butter on one side of each of the bread slices. Place 4 slices of bread, buttered side down, on your work surface. Spread the goat cheese mixture on each slice of bread. Follow with the cheddar and sheep's milk cheese. Top with the remaining bread slices, buttered side up.

For stovetop method: Heat a large nonstick skillet over medium heat for 2 minutes. Put the sandwiches into the pan, cover, and cook for 3 to 4 minutes, until golden brown. Turn the sandwiches, pressing each one firmly with a spatula to flatten slightly. Cover and cook for 3 to 4 minutes, until the undersides are well browned. Remove the cover and turn the sandwiches once more. Press firmly with the spatula again, cook for 1 minute, and remove from the pan. Let cool for 5 minutes. Cut in half and serve.

For sandwich maker method: Preheat the sandwich maker. Follow directions for assembly above. Cook according to manufacturer's instructions.

Makes 4 sandwiches

The Wisconsinite

Wisconsin isn't called the Dairy State for nothing. It is the largest cheese-producing state in the nation, the place where Colby cheese was invented, and it boasts 46 different blue cheeses alone. In addition to cheese, Wisconsin produces cranberries, which is the number-one fruit crop there. Furthermore, the state is also home to the Mustard Museum, in Middleton. I decided to take these disparate elements and put them together between two slices of dark bread (another often used food item in Wisconsin). I love the sweet, tangy, and earthy combination of flavors that results.

- ¼ cup cranberry sauce
- 4 teaspoons Dijon mustard (or use a Wisconsin mustard if you can)
- 2 tablespoons butter, at room temperature
- 8 sandwich-size slices dark rye or marble bread
- 8 ounces Colby cheese (or use Colby-Jack or cheddar)
- 2 ounces blue cheese (such as Hook's Cheese Company Hook's Blue or Seymour Dairy Products Ader Käse), coarsely crumbled (or use any creamy yet slightly crumbly blue cheese)

In a small bowl, mix the cranberry sauce and mustard together.

To assemble: Spread the butter on one side of each slice of bread. Place 4 slices of bread, buttered side down, on your work surface. Spread the cranberry mixture on the bread. Distribute the colby, and crumble the blue cheese over the colby. Top with the remaining bread slices, buttered side up.

For stovetop method: Heat a large nonstick skillet over medium heat for 2 minutes. Put the sandwiches into the pan, cover, and cook for 2 to 3 minutes, until the undersides have darkened and become crisp. Turn the

sandwiches, pressing each one firmly with a spatula to flatten slightly. Cover and cook for 2 to 3 minutes, until the undersides are crisp. Remove the cover, turn the sandwiches once more, and press firmly with the spatula once again. Cook for 1 minute, or until the cheese has melted completely. (You might have to peek inside to make sure.) Remove from the pan and let cool for 5 minutes. Cut in half and serve.

For sandwich maker method: Preheat the sandwich maker. Follow directions for assembly above. Cook according to manufacturer's instructions.

Makes 4 sandwiches

Chapter 8

old favorites and modern sides

Ultimate Childhood Flashback

You might not want to admit it, but I'll bet you ate a version of this sandwich at some point in your life. Perhaps you still do. All I know is that the crunchy and salty potato chips *inside* the sandwich create a decadent sensation that is every bit as appealing to our adult selves as it is to the child in us.

2 tablespoons butter, at room temperature

8 slices white bread

2 tablespoons mayonnaise

8 (1-ounce) slices American cheese

8 medium dill pickles, sliced lengthwise into thirds

2 ounces potato chips

To assemble: Spread the butter on one side of each of the bread slices. Place 4 slices of bread, buttered side down, on your work surface. Spread the mayonnaise on each slice of bread. Follow with 1 slice of cheese. Lay the pickle slices on the cheese. Place a few chips on top of the pickles and follow with the remaining slices of cheese. Top with the remaining bread slices, buttered side up.

For stovetop method: Heat a large nonstick skillet over medium heat for 2 minutes. Put the sandwiches into the pan, cover, and cook for 2 to 3 minutes, until golden brown. Turn the sandwiches, pressing each one lightly with a spatula to flatten slightly (you don't want to crush the potato chips to smithereens). Cover and cook for 5 minutes, or until the undersides are well browned. Turn the sandwiches once more, press firmly with the spatula again, cook for 1 minute, and remove from the pan. Let cool for 2 to 3 minutes. Cut in half and serve.

For sandwich maker method: Preheat the sandwich maker. Follow directions for assembly above. Cook according to manufacturer's instructions.

Makes 4 sandwiches

Dutch Treat

Anneke Scholten, a manager of Aspen, Colorado's restaurant Montagna, remembers eating this sandwich while growing up in her Dutch household. It may sound strange to many of us, but if you like bananas, you'll discover that cheese with banana isn't such an odd combination after all. The brûlée effect that happens once the sugar meets the heat seals the deal, making this a great breakfast or dessert sandwich.

* * *

1 tablespoon butter, at room temperature

4 slices country white or wheat bread

1½ bananas, peeled and sliced ¼ inch thick

8 ounces aged Gouda cheese, coarsely grated

2 teaspoons brown sugar

Place an oven rack 6 inches below the heating element and preheat the broiler.

To assemble: Butter one side of each piece of bread. Place the bread on a broiler pan or baking sheet, buttered side up, and toast on one side. Turn the bread, toasted side down. Cover the surface of the bread with the banana slices. Distribute the cheese, compressing with your hand if necessary to keep the cheese from falling over the sides of the bread. Crumble the sugar over the cheese.

Broil until the cheese is golden brown and bubbly, about 5 minutes. Let cool slightly and serve.

NOTE: Because the sandwich is open-face, it cannot be made in a sandwich maker.

Makes 4 sandwiches

Toast Hawaii

When a German chef told me that the grilled cheese sandwich he grew up with was called Toast Hawaii, I decided to look into it. Speculation is that it may have been modeled after a Grilled Spamwich, invented by the Spam folks and brought to Germany by U.S. Army troops. However, a German TV food host in the 1950s is credited with inventing the postwar version of this open-face sandwich. His called for a cherry on top, which you're welcome to include.

- -

8 slices egg bread (or use challah or brioche)

2 tablespoons butter, at room temperature

4 (1-ounce) slices ham

4 (¼-inch-thick) slices fresh or canned pineapple, drained

4 maraschino cherries (optional)

8 ounces Swiss cheese, coarsely grated (or use Gruyère or Emmentaler)

Place an oven rack 6 inches below the heating element and preheat the broiler.

To assemble: Put the bread on a baking sheet. Spread each slice with the butter and place in the broiler to toast. Watch carefully, because egg bread burns easily. Remove from the broiler, turn the slices, and let cool slightly. Layer the ham on top, followed by the pineapple. Place the cherries in the hole of the pineapple and top with the cheese. Broil until the cheese is brown and bubbly, 4 to 5 minutes. Serve right away.

NOTE: Because the sandwich is open-face, it cannot be made in a sandwich maker.

Makes 4 sandwiches

Pictured with Deep-Fried Pickles (page 142)

Erika's PB & Cheese

To be blunt, this sandwich sounds perfectly awful. Peanut butter? Bologna? Really? But this is a favorite of a colleague from Rogue Creamery in Oregon. Although even she cringes at the memory, she also realizes there may be more to it than just a bite of nostalgia. I hate to admit it, but I agree. See for yourself. I dare ya.

- -

4 slices bologna

2 tablespoons mayonnaise

8 sandwich slices whole wheat bread

½ cup crunchy peanut butter

8 ounces Colby cheese, coarsely grated (or use mild cheddar or American)

4 medium kosher dill pickles, cut into thirds lengthwise (or use sandwich stackers)

Heat a large nonstick skillet over medium heat for 2 minutes. Make a small "x" in the middle of the bologna slices to prevent them from curling. Add the bologna to the skillet and cook for about 3 minutes on each side, or until the bologna is well browned. Remove the bologna from the pan and let cool. Wipe out the skillet with a paper towel but do not wash it.

To assemble: Spread the mayonnaise on one side of each of the bread slices. Place 4 slices of bread, mayonnaise side down, on your work surface. Spread 2 tablespoons peanut butter on each slice of bread. Follow with 1 bologna slice and the cheese. Lay the pickle slices on top of the cheese. Top with the remaining bread slices, mayonnaise side up.

For stovetop method: Heat a large nonstick skillet over medium heat for 2 minutes. Put the sandwiches into the pan, cover, and cook for 2 to 3 minutes, until golden brown. Turn the sandwiches, pressing each one firmly with a spatula to flatten slightly. Cover and cook for 2 to 3 minutes, until the undersides are well browned. Turn the sandwiches once more, press firmly with the spatula again, cook for 1 minute, and remove from the pan. Let cool for 5 minutes. Cut in half and serve.

For sandwich maker method: Preheat the sandwich maker. Follow directions for assembly above. Cook according to manufacturer's instructions.

Makes 4 sandwiches

Pickled Cucumbers

Because of the richness of a grilled cheese sandwich, a pickled component not only tastes good, but it's also refreshing. Use these cucumbers wherever you might use pickles. If you decide to put the cucumbers on a sandwich, be sure to drain them well. Otherwise your sandwich will be soggy.

¼ cup cider vinegar

¼ cup water

2 tablespoons sugar

1 teaspoon salt

1 teaspoon finely chopped fresh dill (optional)

1 English cucumber, peeled and sliced ⅛ to ¼ inch thick

In a medium bowl, stir together the vinegar, water, sugar, salt, and dill. Add the cucumbers and stir to coat. Let sit for at least 15 minutes and up to 2 hours. (The cucumbers can be prepared up to 1 day in advance and refrigerated. Bring to room temperature before using.) These can be kept for up to 3 days refrigerated.

SERVE WITH:

Havarti with Balsamic-Glazed Carrots (page 67)

Arepas with Monterey Jack, Plantains, and Black Beans (page 83)

Classic with a Twist (page 20)

Hog Island Grilled Cheese (page 16)

Provençal-Style Grilled Cheese (page 14)

Sweet and Spicy Chicken and Gouda (page 28)

Makes about 1½ cups

Grilled Tomato Soup

For this soup, I use the word *grilled* even though the tomatoes are actually broiled. That's because in some parts of the world, the broiler is actually called the grill. The main point is that the tomatoes get a nice char before they're turned into soup, which makes for sweeter and more complex flavors.

- -

3 pounds Roma tomatoes, cored and halved lengthwise (or use any juicy variety of seasonal tomato)

2 tablespoons olive oil

Salt and freshly ground black pepper

4 tablespoons butter

1 large onion, coarsely chopped

2 cloves garlic, coarsely chopped

2 tablespoons tomato paste

2 (3-inch) sprigs thyme

2 small sprigs basil with leaves (about 5 leaves on each sprig)

½ cup vegetable or chicken stock or water, plus more as needed

Place an oven rack about 6 inches below the heating element and preheat the broiler.

Put the tomatoes, cut side up, on a rimmed baking sheet. Drizzle with olive oil, and sprinkle with salt and pepper. Broil until the tomatoes are bubbly, charred in places, and somewhat sunken, 8 to 10 minutes.

Meanwhile, place 2 tablespoons of the butter in a large nonstick skillet over medium heat. Add the onion and cook, stirring occasionally, until limp, 5 to 6 minutes. Add the garlic and stir constantly until softened.

Transfer the tomatoes to the skillet, juice and all. Add the tomato paste, thyme, and basil and cook over medium heat, breaking up the tomatoes with a wooden spoon, until the flavors begin to meld, about 5 minutes.

Remove the herbs and transfer the mixture to a food processor. Add the stock and remaining 2 tablespoons of butter, and process until smooth. Taste and add salt and pepper as needed. If the mixture is too thick, add additional stock or water 2 tablespoons at a time.

Makes 4 to 5 cups, depending on the amount of liquid you add at the end, and serves 4 people

Deep-Fried Pickles

Once again, chef Ryan Hardy's brilliance strikes. Unlike his Italian-style sandwich *Due Due* (page 5), this is as down-home Americana as it gets. Serve these pickles with just about any sandwich you'd like, although you might be tempted to eat them all by themselves.

Although you can use regular all-purpose flour, I highly recommend using the cake flour specified here because of the lighter and airier coating it creates. Alternatively, you can use instant flour, most often found under the brand name Wondra, which will yield similar results.

½ cup cake flour
2½ tablespoons cornstarch
1½ teaspoons baking powder
¾ teaspoon salt
½ cup cold sparkling water
Vegetable oil, for frying
1 cup dill pickle chips, drained and patted dry

In a medium bowl, whisk together the flour, cornstarch, baking powder, and salt until well-mixed and free of lumps. Slowly whisk in the sparkling water, whisking until smooth. The mixture should have the consistency of pancake batter. If it's too thick, add a little more sparkling water as needed. Refrigerate until ready to cook.

Line a rimmed baking sheet with paper towels and set a wire rack over it.

Pour oil into a deep heavy skillet to a depth of ¾ inch. Heat over medium-high heat until shimmering. To determine if the oil is ready, sprinkle a pinch of flour into the oil. It should sizzle immediately and slowly brown.

Lightly and evenly coat the pickle chips with the batter. Lift them out of the batter with a fork or tongs so that the excess batter can drip away. Lower a few pickles at a time into the oil. They should be able to float freely. Fry the pickles until golden brown, turning once, about 2 minutes per side, adjusting the heat as needed. (The oil should continue to sizzle, but not pop.) Drain on the wire rack and serve warm.

SERVE WITH:
Creamy, Cheesy, and Smoky Croissant (page 51)
Cubano (page 87)
Hog Island Grilled Cheese (page 16)
Classic with a Twist (page 20)
Shepherd Sandwich with Ham and Tomato (page 59)
French Mountain Glory (page 36)
Smoky Kim-Cheese (page 34)
The Wisconsinite (page 128)
Erika's PB & Cheese (page 137)
Ultimate Childhood Flashback (page 132)

Makes about 2 dozen

Mostarda di Mediterranea

This recipe was created by Ryan Hardy to serve as an accompaniment for his sandwich *Due Due* (see page 5). It makes much more than you'll need for one batch of sandwiches, but luckily the *mostarda* lasts for a month refrigerated and can be used for more than just grilled cheese sandwiches. Try it with charcuterie or grilled chicken or pork, or top olive oil–brushed crostini with goat cheese and a small dollop of the *mostarda* for a terrific hors d'oeuvre.

1¼ cups sugar

1 (1.75-ounce) package fruit pectin

1 pound red bell peppers, seeded and coarsely chopped

½ cup cider vinegar

¾ teaspoon red pepper flakes

½ teaspoon kosher salt

¼ cup freshly squeezed lemon juice (from about 1 large lemon)

In a small bowl, whisk together ¼ cup of the sugar and the pectin. Set aside.

Place the bell peppers in the bowl of a food processor and process until finely chopped. The mixture will be somewhat liquefied, with pieces of pepper distributed throughout. Transfer to a medium saucepan and add the vinegar, red pepper flakes, and salt. Bring to a boil, and then decrease the heat to a simmer. Cook, stirring occasionally, for 10 minutes. Add the lemon juice and the remaining 1 cup sugar, and stir until the sugar has dissolved. Bring to a boil again, and whisk in the sugar-pectin mixture. Stir constantly for 1 minute. Remove from the heat, transfer to a bowl, and cool completely. (The *mostarda* can be made up to 1 month ahead of time. Place in a clean jar and refrigerate.)

SERVE WITH:

Due Due (page 5)

Hog Island Grilled Cheese (page 16)

Shepherd Sandwich with Ham and Tomato (page 59)

Sweet and Spicy Chicken and Gouda (page 28)

Italian Melt (page 32)

French Mountain Glory (page 36)

Alpine Grilled Cheese with Pickled Shallots and Watercress (page 75)

Makes about 2 cups

Apple-Onion Chutney

Because of its sweet-tart nature, chutney is a wonderful accompaniment to cheese, especially cheddar. Try this chutney with any of the sandwiches that would seem as if their flavors would be lifted by a little sweetness and acidity. Because this makes a lot of chutney, you might also go beyond grilled cheese and serve it with pork or grilled chicken.

1 cup cider vinegar

¼ cup packed plus 2 tablespoons light brown sugar, plus more as needed

1 pound Granny Smith apples, peeled, cored, and diced

½ large yellow onion, coarsely chopped (about ¾ cup)

⅓ cup golden raisins

2 cloves garlic, minced

Zest from 1 lemon, grated (about 1½ tablespoons)

2 tablespoons freshly squeezed lemon juice (from about ½ lemon)

⅛ teaspoon red pepper flakes, or more to taste

¾ teaspoon yellow mustard seed

Pinch of salt

In a medium heavy saucepan, combine the vinegar and brown sugar and bring to a boil. Cook until the mixture is reduced by about one-third, 5 to 10 minutes. Add the apples, onion, raisins, garlic, lemon zest and juice, red pepper flakes, mustard seed, and salt. Stir the ingredients together, turn the heat to a low simmer, cover, and cook, stirring occasionally, for 45 to 55 minutes, until most of the liquid has cooked away, the apples are soft, and the vinegar has mellowed. You may need to add a little more brown sugar to get the proper sweet-sour balance. The mixture should be thick.

To bring out the best flavor, let the chutney sit for at least 2 hours at room temperature before serving. Or cover and refrigerate for up to 2 weeks. Bring to room temperature before serving.

NOTE: If the mixture seems dry as it cooks, add water 2 tablespoons at a time. Conversely, if it seems too moist, place the lid slightly ajar to allow some of the liquid to cook away.

SERVE WITH:
Cubano (page 87)
Welsh Rarebit (page 78)
Say *Oui* to Normandy (page 27)
Sweet-Tart Cheddar and Chorizo (page 25)

Makes about 2 cups

Tomato Jam

This recipe is based on one I got years ago from Charles Dale, now the chef at Encantado Resort in Santa Fe. Although I don't think Charles had grilled cheese sandwiches in mind when he created the recipe, I feel pretty certain he'd wholeheartedly approve of its use for just that purpose. Note that you can make this a week in advance and refrigerate it. Also, you'll have more jam than you need for one batch of sandwiches. You can use the extra to make more sandwiches, and it's also great with salmon or on hamburgers.

6 large ripe tomatoes (about 1½ pounds) peeled, seeded, and coarsely chopped (use fresh Roma tomatoes if it isn't tomato season or one 28-ounce can of peeled Roma or San Marzano tomatoes, drained and seeds removed)

1 clove garlic, finely chopped

¼ cup red wine vinegar

2½ tablespoons sugar (if you're making this in the middle of tomato season when tomatoes are at their sweetest, reduce the sugar by 1 to 2 teaspoons)

Salt

Place all the ingredients in a medium saucepan over medium-low heat. The mixture should bubble ever so slightly but not boil. Cook for about 1 hour, or until the jam has thickened and most of the liquid has evaporated. Let cool. (You can make this up to 1 week in advance. Store in the refrigerator.)

SERVE WITH:
Double Cheddar and Tomato Jam (page 9)
Welsh Rarebit (page /8)
Hog Island Grilled Cheese (page 16)
Provençal-Style Grilled Cheese (page 14)
Spinach, Egg, and Manchego (page 2)
Classic with a Twist (page 20)
Arepas with Monterey Jack, Plantains, and Black Beans (page 83)

Makes about ¾ cup

Appendix:
Where Grilled Cheese Plays the Starring Role

Arkansas
Hammontree's Gourmet Grilled Cheese
   Sandwiches*
Fayetteville
www.hammontreesgourmet.com

California
Campanile—Grilled Cheese Night (Thursdays)
Los Angeles
www.campanilerestaurant.com

Cheese Plus
San Francisco
www.cheeseplus.com

Clementine Bakery
Los Angeles
www.clementineonline.com

Greenspan's Grilled Cheese
Los Angeles
(Web site not yet determined at print time)

Sidekick (Cowgirl Creamery)
San Francisco
www.cowgirlcreamery.com

The American Grilled Cheese Kitchen*
San Francisco
www.theamericansf.com

The Grilled Cheese Truck*
Los Angeles
www.thegrilledcheesetruck.com

'wichcraft
San Francisco
www.wichcraftnyc.com

Colorado
Chez Cheese Gourmet Market
Denver
www.facebook.com/pages/Denver-CO/Chez-
Cheese-Gourmet-Market/90669959859

Connecticut
Grilled Cheese To Go
Milford
www.grilledcheesetogo.com

Florida
Grilligan's Grilled Cheese
Vero Beach
www.grilligans.wavebutler.com

The Cheese Course (several locations)
Weston
www.thecheesecourse.com

Georgia
Republic Social House
Atlanta
www.republicsocialhouse.com

Illinois
Pastoral Artisan Cheese, Bread, Wine (three
   locations)
Chicago
www.pastoralartisan.com

Maryland
Grilled Cheese & Company*
Catonsville
www.ilovegrilledcheese.com

The Mt. Washington Tavern
Baltimore
www.mtwashingtontavern.com

Massachusetts
Grilled Cheese Tuesdays at Dante
Cambridge
www.restaurantdante.com

Roxy's Gourmet Grilled Cheese (mobile truck)
Boston
twitter.com/roxysgrilledchz

Rubi's Coffee & Sandwiches
Great Barrington
www.facebook.com/pages/Great-Barrington-
MA/rubis-coffee-sandwiches/349668086893

Michigan
Grilled Cheese and Tomato Soup
Farmington Hills
www.gcatsoup.com

The Panini Press
Berkley
www.thepaninipress.com

Nevada
Dad's Grilled Cheese
Las Vegas
www.dadsgrilledcheese.com

'wichcraft
Las Vegas
www.wichcraftnyc.com

New Jersey
Grilled Cheese and Crab Cake Co.
Somers Point
www.grilledcheeseandcrabcakeatlantic.com

The Pop Shop
Collingswood
www.thepopshopusa.com

New York
'ino Café/Bar
New York City
www.cafeino.com

Murray's Cheese
New York City
www.murrayscheese.com

The Milk Truck*
New York City/Brooklyn
www.milktruckgrilledcheese.com

'wichcraft (several locations)
New York City
www.wichcraftnyc.com

Ohio
Melt Bar & Grilled (two locations)
Cleveland
www.meltbarandgrilled.com

Melt Eclectic Deli
Cincinnati
www.meltcincy.com

Tom + Chee
Cincinnati
http://www.facebook.com/4TomAndChee

Oregon
The Grilled Cheese Grill*
Portland
www.grilledcheesegrill.com

Savor Soup House (make-your-own-grilled-
   cheese bar)
Portland
www.savorsouphouse.com

South Dakota
Chedd's Gourmet Grilled Cheese
Sioux Falls
www.chedds.com

Texas
Austin Daily Press
Austin (mobile truck)
www.austindailypress.com

Chedd's Gourmet Grilled Cheese
Austin
www.chedds.com

Washington
Beecher's Handmade Cheese
Seattle
www.beechershandmadecheese.com

*Featured in the Grilled Cheese on the Go chapter

Metric Conversions and Equivalents

Metric Conversion Formulas

TO CONVERT	MULTIPLY
Ounces to grams	Ounces by 28.35
Pounds to kilograms	Pounds by .454
Teaspoons to milliliters	Teaspoons by 4.93
Tablespoons to milliliters	Tablespoons by 14.79
Fluid ounces to milliliters	Fluid ounces by 29.57
Cups to milliliters	Cups by 236.59
Cups to liters	Cups by .236
Pints to liters	Pints by .473
Quarts to liters	Quarts by .946
Gallons to liters	Gallons by 3.785
Inches to centimeters	Inches by 2.54

Approximate Metric Equivalents

VOLUME

¼ teaspoon	1 milliliter
½ teaspoon	2.5 milliliters
¾ teaspoon	4 milliliters
1 teaspoon	5 milliliters
1¼ teaspoons	6 milliliters
1½ teaspoons	7.5 milliliters
1¾ teaspoons	8.5 milliliters
2 teaspoons	10 milliliters
1 tablespoon (½ fluid ounce)	15 milliliters
2 tablespoons (1 fluid ounce)	30 milliliters
¼ cup	60 milliliters
⅓ cup	80 milliliters
½ cup (4 fluid ounces)	120 milliliters
⅔ cup	160 milliliters
¾ cup	180 milliliters
1 cup (8 fluid ounces)	240 milliliters
1 ¼ cups	300 milliliters
1½ cups (12 fluid ounces)	360 milliliters
1⅔ cups	400 milliliters
2 cups (1 pint)	460 milliliters
3 cups	700 milliliters
4 cups (1 quart)	.95 liter
1 quart plus ¼ cup	1 liter
4 quarts (1 gallon)	3.8 liters

WEIGHT

¼ ounce	7 grams
½ ounce	14 grams
¾ ounce	21 grams
1 ounce	28 grams
1¼ ounces	35 grams
1½ ounces	42.5 grams
1⅔ ounces	45 grams
2 ounces	57 grams
3 ounces	85 grams
4 ounces (¼ pound)	113 grams
5 ounces	142 grams
6 ounces	170 grams
7 ounces	198 grams
8 ounces (½ pound)	227 grams
16 ounces (1 pound)	454 grams
35.25 ounces (2.2 pounds)	1 kilogram

LENGTH

⅛ inch	3 millimeters
¼ inch	6 millimeters
½ inch	1¼ centimeters
1 inch	2½ centimeters
2 inches	5 centimeters
2½ inches	6 centimeters
4 inches	10 centimeters
5 inches	13 centimeters
6 inches	15¼ centimeters
12 inches (1 foot)	30 centimeters

Information compiled from a variety of sources, including *Recipes into Type* by Joan Whitman and Dolores Simon (Newton, MA: Biscuit Books, 2000); *The New Food Lover's Companion* by Sharon Tyler Herbst (Hauppauge, NY: Barron's, 1995); and *Rosemary Brown's Big Kitchen Instruction Book* (Kansas City, MO: Andrews McMeel, 1998).

Index